∞

Christians Courageous

Also by Aloysius Roche
from Sophia Institute Press®:

A Bedside Book of Saints

Christians Courageous

by Aloysius Roche

Illustrated by Antony Lake

SOPHIA INSTITUTE PRESS®
Manchester, New Hampshire

Christians Courageous was formerly published by Sheed and Ward, New York, in 1955. This 2009 edition by Sophia Institute Press® contains minor revisions.

Copyright © 2009 Sophia Institute Press®

Printed in the United States of America

All rights reserved

Cover design by Theodore Schluenderfritz

On the cover: *The Naval Battle of Lepanto*, by Juan Luna y Novicio / The Bridgeman Art Library International.

Sophia Institute Press®
Box 5284, Manchester, NH 03108
1-800-888-9344
www.sophiainstitute.com

Nihil obstat: Georgius Smith, S.T.D., Ph.D., *Censor Deputatus*
Imprimatur: E. Morrogh Bernard, *Vicarius Generalis*
Westmonasterii, September 4, 1954

Library of Congress Cataloging-in-Publication Data

Roche, Aloysius, b. 1886.
    Christians courageous / by Aloysius Roche ; Illustrated by
      Antony Lake.
      p. cm.
    Originally published: New York : Sheed and Ward, 1955.
    ISBN 978-1-933184-54-8 (pbk. : alk. paper) 1. Christian
      biography. I. Title.
    BR1703.R6 2009
    270.092'2 — dc22
    [B]
                                     2009016536

09 10 11 12 13 14 9 8 7 6 5 4 3 2 1

∞

Contents

∞

∞

Preface

Although the word *hero* has come down to us from classical times, it would be a mistake to infer that heroism was a monopoly of the ancients, or that the propagation of the gospel tended to make life tame and humdrum, to diminish the stature of persons and of events. There are few pages of Christian history that do not afford an emphatic refutation of that particular error. Our Savior did advise us to learn a lesson from the birds of the air and the flowers of the field, a lesson of detachment and other-worldliness; and, no doubt, at the time, there were those ready to argue that the successful preaching of such a gospel was bound to weaken the fibers of human endeavor and create a weak-kneed and timorous sort of society. But these precepts were not the whole of the story. There were other texts besides, challenging and provocative appeals addressed to the combative and adventurous element in our nature, all culminating in a command as peremptory as the crack of a whip: Go into the whole world and teach all nations.

And, sure enough, in due course, along came the Wind of Pentecost, and this seems to have produced and multiplied that hurricane type of individual, exemplified in St. Paul, to whom all obstacles, no matter how formidable, exist only in order that they may be surmounted or swept aside. Foremost among the marvels of that first Pentecost was the newly found fearlessness of the men who emerged from the upper room to begin the work of the apostolate. And this fearlessness, a nine days' growth, was no mere nine days' wonder. It had come to stay, apparently, and it was destined to become current-coin, so to say, to circulate freely among the rank-and-file, among those whom St. Francis called the *little people*. The early Christian centuries were pre-eminently the Age of the Martyrs and, in the persons of these martyrs, the pagan authorities were astonished to see the mere rabble climbing onto the pedestals heretofore reserved for the well-born or highly placed. It soon became evident that these Galileans were not to be sneered at, that they were extremists by profession, committed to hazards and hardships, bent on making history, determined to shape their world to what they believed to be a God-given mold.

Strong reasons make strong actions. The actions that stirred the ancient world were certainly inspired by strong enough reasons; but these strong reasons were not always either high-minded or morally sound. The new reasons that issued out of Palestine were made doubly strong by being good ones, and by having their roots in eternity; so strong were they that they have produced a succession of enterprises as daring as any to be found in the more-or-less fanciful pages of Virgil or Homer.

Some of these enterprises are brought to life again in *Christians Courageous*, and brought to life in the form of stories which, while respecting the historical facts, have provided a certain amount of scope for the play of the imagination. Written primarily for youthful readers, they may at the same time prove acceptable to all those to whom the achievements of their religious forefathers are a matter of pride and encouragement.

∞

Christians Courageous

∞

Ardalion the Actor

Diocletian was one of those who begin at the bottom and end at the top. His parents were slaves, and he himself entered the Roman army as a private soldier. But his abilities were such that, in the year 284, he was proclaimed emperor by his comrades while he was still a young man. His long and successful reign was marred by a violent persecution of the Christians, for which Galerius, his colleague and subordinate, was mainly responsible.

It is well known that for the space of 250 years, the newly founded Church was harried with fire and sword, and every conceivable instrument of torture. The whole fabric of the Roman state rested on the old idolatry, so that any religious movement, aiming at the overthrow of that idolatry, was regarded as a treasonable movement and treated as such.

This explains why even fair-minded and tolerant rulers, such as Marcus Aurelius and Pius Antoninus, initiated stern measures against the adherents of the new Faith. They took their stand upon the laws, one of the most ancient of which forbade, under penalty of death, the worship of any god not approved by the Senate. There were other charges besides, mostly false. Indeed, slanderous accusations so multiplied that anyone could see that the authorities had determined to exterminate the new sect, by fair means or foul.

These official proscriptions, like the plagues of Egypt, were ten in number; and it is calculated that, while they persisted, something like five million men, women, and children were put to death. The first occurred under Nero and the last under Diocletian; and this last was in many ways one of the worst of all.

To begin with, the number of victims was enormous, including Alban, a native of Britain, and that famous soldier, George by name, who is the acknowledged patron of a number of countries, including England. Seventeen thousand were sacrificed in the first month. In Egypt, at that time the most Christian part of the empire, the martyrdoms were so continuous that the public executioners were worn out with the work of slaughter. To make matters worse, savage cruelties were practiced on the bodies of the martyrs before they were put to death. For example, the brave man who tore down the edict, or proclamation, announcing the persecution was roasted alive over a slow fire.

Still, notwithstanding the grievousness of the trials that beset them, Christians everywhere were in better heart than at any time since the fury of the state was first let loose against them. Then they were hopelessly outnumbered by a pagan population united in an active hatred of all that they stood for; now they had multiplied to such an extent that their extermination would have brought the machinery of government to a standstill. It is calculated that at least one-twentieth of the subjects owing allegiance to the Roman power had enrolled themselves under the banner of the Cross around this time. Whole districts, in Africa especially, were Christian, while in the capital itself there must have been close upon two hundred thousand professing the faith of the gospel.

Over and above, the people at large could no longer be counted on to swallow the lying catchwords of the government. Public opinion was, on the whole, friendly to the Christians and hostile to the political measures devised for their undoing. This the Christians were well aware of, and they nerved themselves to sustain what they felt confident would be their final ordeal.

The persecution of Diocletian, however, was bitter enough, and when it was at the height of its fury, there was one individual in the capital who resolved to exploit the situation to his own advantage. This was Ardalion, a Greek by birth and an actor by profession. Ardalion specialized in that particular branch of dramatic entertainment known as the mime. He had inherited the tradition of his countrymen, among whom, in Sicily especially, this artistic form had been developed during centuries. Long practice had so perfected his powers that theater-goers were of the opinion that Ardalion actually became, for the time being, the individual whom he was impersonating. More than once his life had been threatened by the exasperated victims of his mimicry.

Among the Romans, the prejudice against acting was very deep-seated, and in the profession, Greeks far outnumbered the natives. It was not until the end of the republic that anything like a permanent building was erected for purely theatrical purposes. The people sought their entertainment in the circuses and amphitheaters, where spectacles were staged, or in variety shows exhibiting rope-dancers, conjurers, boxers, clowns, stilt-walkers, and contortionists. These centers of recreation, like our parks, were open to the public. In all places where Roman civilization has left its mark, it is the amphitheater that characterizes the city, just as it is the theater that characterizes the Greek city. Real plays do not appear to have been popular in Italy, but the mime was the exception, at any rate for a period. Its inventors, the Greeks, presented it as something grave and dignified, but with the Romans it was mostly buffoonery, a kind of acted satire on some topic of the day. This had given Ardalion his chance, and in this particular line he was unrivaled.

Of late, however, the popularity of the great actor had been on the wane. His supporters were getting tired of the shows he was putting on and were looking around for something in the shape of a novelty. Ardalion, therefore, determined upon a bold course. He resolved to stage a series of performances in which he would parody the beliefs and practices of the Christian Faith, and follow this up with a mock trial, in which a Christian priest would be arraigned and cross-examined as a traitor to the state and to the majesty of the emperor.

Outsider though he was, these beliefs and practices were by no means unfamiliar to him. Some of his best friends were professing Christians; and, in spite of the fact that they were apt to be reticent concerning their religious affairs, these affairs were, nevertheless, fairly well known. Educated pagans like him had access to the tribunals, where Christians of every rank were daily charged with conspiracy before being put to death. By means of these cross-examinations, in which the victims boldly professed and defended their faith, it was possible to acquire a fairly accurate knowledge of their habits and tenets.

Ardalion, however, was not the man to leave anything to chance. As an additional security, he looked for, and soon found, a certain renegade Christian who, for a consideration, undertook to coach him in the business he was going to put on the stage. For weeks the two worked together in secret until, at last, the quick-witted Ardalion, with his faultless memory, had so familiarized himself with the matters in hand that he might have passed for one of the initiated. And whereas formerly he had dropped into the courts casually and out of mere curiosity, he now made a point of attending regularly. He studied the demeanor of the prisoners; he made notes of their answers and speeches; and all that he thus learned during the day, he rehearsed far into the night.

The upshot of all was that, one morning, the citizens of Rome found parchments displayed about the city, advertising the appearance of their favorite in a new role, designed to expose to the light of day the mysteries of the now-extinct sect of infidels known as Christians. This strangely worded announcement was intended to tally with recent government proclamations, to the effect that the measures taken against the Christian Faith had already resulted in its extermination.

On the opening night, Ardalion was conscious of a strange sensation. Excitement he was used to, but this was something different. Anxiety he was used to as well, and he was aware that this new venture of his would be decisive of his future, for good or ill. No, it was not that either; he knew his own powers and felt sure of surpassing himself. Firm believer in Fate that he was, he vaguely felt that destiny had marked him down for something momentous, that this was to be the turning point of his career.

The twelve-foot-long stage, or proscenium, was flanked by the wings, through which the actors made their exits and entrances, and backed by the *skene*, or scene, a long stretch of canvas attached to a portable frame. On this was depicted a representation in keeping with the action of the play. At the extremities of the stage was a revolving apparatus carrying three different side scenes, each of which could be put in position at a moment's notice.

By the time the doors were opened, Ardalion was dressed and ready for the part he was about to play. For a while, he paced restlessly to and fro behind the *skene*, and then he took up a position at the eyelet through which he was able to watch the spectators filing into the building. A special section was set apart for women, and Ardalion could see them moving into their places, carrying large cushions, which they used partly for sitting on and partly as a protection against the feet of the spectators sitting immediately behind. The audience came in through passages on each side of the stage, and then mounted the stone steps leading to the tiers that, in the case of this theater, were arranged fan-wise so as to form a perfect semicircle with its center looking straight at the stage. The orchestra was situated on the floor level immediately in front of the stage, which could be reached by means of a flight of stairs. In niches around the auditorium, bronze vessels were set to act as amplifiers or loudspeakers. They were going to be needed, for already the house was filled to capacity.

Presently, the customary signal was given, and the chatter of the audience died away. Ardalion, who knew all that there was to be known about the show-business, had arranged his performance in such a way that the preliminary scenes led up, one by one, to the catastrophe or climax of the performance. Into this culminating act he meant to put the best of himself and of his art.

And so the first scenes showed a number of pagans undergoing examination and then being initiated into the mysteries of the Christian Faith. Care was taken to represent these as mean and poverty-stricken individuals, belonging to the lowest orders of society, as though the proscribed religion drew its recruits only from the servile and criminal classes — an insinuation in strict accord with official propaganda, but one that everybody knew to be false. These representations were gone through rather hurriedly and were of little interest to the spectators as a whole. They were followed by an attempt to reproduce the central service of the Christian Church, Ardalion taking the part of the officiating president with the lesser clergy in attendance. But here again the representation was clumsy and could be properly appreciated only by those in the audience, and there were many such, who were or had been Christians.

Over and above, there were signs of disappointment, at any rate on the part of some of the pagans among the spectators. In Italy, and especially in Rome, miming was expected to be a funny business, something in the nature of a burlesque. So far, however, the performance had maintained a uniform level of dignity and respect. Still, it was generally understood that these sketches were meant only to serve as an introduction to the main piece, in which the actor was expected to excel himself. Great, therefore, was the excitement when at last the Christians' meeting was broken up by the officers of the law, and Ardalion was arrested and led away to face his trial before no less a tribunal than the Roman Senate itself. These final proceedings were to occupy the greater part of the time allotted to the show.

In the interval that followed, as the stage was being rearranged, Ardalion retired to his dressing room, obviously abstracted and ill at ease. Although his subordinates knew from experience that he always insisted on playing his parts to the life, it seemed odd that he should maintain his seriousness even behind the scenes, where it was customary for everybody to relax. To all attempts to draw him into conversation he made but one reply: "Let everything be done according to our arrangement." Speculation was cut short by the warning signal, and the performers filed onto the stage for the concluding act, which was to tax the memory of the two principals to the utmost. These were Ardalion himself, playing the part of the Christian bishop on trial for his life, and Ardalion's colleague Crescentius, playing the part of the presiding magistrate or judge.

A preliminary interrogation having been gone through, the judge asked the prisoner if he knew the contents of the late edicts issued by the emperors. To this Ardalion answered in the negative, adding, "If these edicts are designed to make me other than I am, then they have no interest for me. I am a Christian, edicts or no edicts."

Judge: The emperors have commanded all without exception to sacrifice to the gods.

Ardalion: It is not possible for me to offer sacrifice to those in whose existence I do not believe.

Judge: Do you not know that there are gods?

Ardalion: No.

Judge: Well, I shall make you know it shortly.

Ardalion: I know that there is one God, who made heaven and earth and all things therein. That God, and Him only, I believe in and adore.

Judge: Do you not consider it a disgraceful thing in a Roman citizen that he should refuse to worship the gods of Rome?

Ardalion: No. Your own poets have been at pains to prove that these same gods are unworthy of our respect and certainly of our love. If your worship is not sincere, it is a thing of no worth. And how can one offer a sincere worship to those whom it is impossible either to respect or to love? But your own poets, I say, represent these gods of yours as dissolute, immoral, and cruel; as gods whose recreation it is to cheat and lie and steal, to say nothing of worse crimes than these. You would be very wroth if you discovered that your own son was planning treachery against you. Yet you honor Jupiter, who did that very thing. Now, the God whom I adore, the Christ, was of a character and life so unblemished that He was described as one who went about doing good. And He commanded us, His followers, to model our lives on the example of His life. He bade us exercise restraint over our passions and impulses, to moderate our anger, to cast from us hatred, envy, and revengeful feelings. He taught us to pray for our very enemies and detractors. He taught us to exercise charity, to relieve distress and to comfort those in sorrow. In short, He taught us to obey the laws of conduct laid down by Himself. Your gods, on the other hand, have totally neglected the lives and morals of the people and nations who worship them. Can you name a single occasion when your so-called gods have commanded you to practice virtue?

Judge: By refusing to acknowledge the divinity of the emperors, you are placing yourself outside the laws.

Ardalion: In all things right and lawful you will find us ready to obey your laws; you will find none readier, in truth, for such obedience is part of our religious duty. But in our sacred books it is written that one must worship the God of Heaven, the Lord of creation, and Him only. The emperor is a man, and we are forbidden to give to a man the honor due to God alone. You yourselves have more than once acknowledged the divinity of emperors whom you afterward deposed, branded with disgrace, and put to death. What respect did you show to the majesty of these emperors? If you judge it treasonable in us to refuse to worship Jupiter, Mars, Saturn, and the rest, how comes it to pass that you do not judge it treasonable in the Jews to make the selfsame refusal? The Jews adhere to their national religion, and to their national God, Jehovah. You do not molest them on that account. Even after the destruction of Jerusalem, your laws made no change in the religious status of the Jews; even now they have a full legal right to worship in accordance with their conscience. How are we Christians different from the Jews? Were we, who do not believe in your gods, to go through the pretense of offering them incense and adoration, we would be making a mockery not only of our own religion, but of your religion as well. Many among you scruple not to be guilty of this mockery. Educated men in plenty, among you, officials and functionaries, comply in public with the demands of a religion that, in private, they deride. Such men are applauded as good citizens, while we who refuse to connive at such base deception are branded as traitors.

This statement, which everyone in the audience knew to be a statement of fact, produced a marked effect, and a murmur of approval ran through the building. The occupants of the seats reserved for public officials were seen to be in consultation, while the actors on the stage were plainly disconcerted by the turn things were taking — Crescentius in particular, who was receiving answers to his questions that the rehearsal had not led him to expect.

Ardalion appeared to be carried out of himself, to resemble some oracle uttering things at the dictation of a higher power. A long pause ensued, and it was only with a violent effort that the judge was able to carry on where he had left off. Assuming a more conciliatory tone, he asked the prisoner how old he was, and, on being told, he went on: "You are still quite a young man, and it is hard to die at your age. Are you not afraid of death?"

Ardalion: Death, O Judge, neither you nor I can hope to avoid. And it is no harder to die at thirty-five than at seventy-five. It is no harder to die under the stroke of the executioner than to die of fever, of dysentery or the like. True, I love my life, for there is nothing better than to be alive. But this love of life does not make me abhor death, because this death that you speak of is the gateway leading to the life eternal promised to the soul that has lived well here. The Christ whom I adore taught us this, taught us to look forward to immortality as the reward of our faith in Him.

The judge then asked Ardalion whom he supposed this Christ of his to be.

Ardalion: He was the Son of God and was made man in Judea. His claim to be divine He proved, by the wonders He wrought while alive and by rising from the dead after He had been crucified. Filled with the wisdom of Heaven, He taught us the truth regarding God and regarding ourselves. But He incurred the envy and the enmity of those in power, as did Socrates. Like him, He was unjustly sentenced to death. But although He died, death had no power over Him, and the grave could not keep Him in bondage. He rose from the dead. During the space of forty days, He showed Himself to His followers, not in the dreams of nighttime, but by day and in the

open air. It was then that He spoke to them of the kingdom of God, on the shores of the lake, sitting in the
shade of the trees, on the grass of the hillside. At the
end of forty days, He was raised up from the earth until
the clouds received Him out of sight.

Judge: And where is He now?

Ardalion: He dwells at the right hand of His Father in Heaven.
But He dwells also in the hearts of those who believe in
Him, and are proud to bear His name. *In my heart He
dwells;* yes, even in the heart of such a one as I.

By this time, the actor was like one transfigured. An unearthly
light shone in his pale and handsome features. His eyes took on
the radiance of the stars. Then, when a profound hush had fallen
upon the spectators, he advanced to the front of the stage and
made the declaration that had been hovering upon his lips, almost
from the moment the mock-trial had begun. In clear and simple
tones, he told the audience that his play-acting days were over,
that he had found a better part and intended to play it in dead
earnest and to the end, no matter how bitter an end that end
might be.

"The performance is finished," he said. "What I sought to tri-
umph over by force of mimicry has triumphed over me by force of
its own inherent truth. For years, I have diverted and amused you
with deceptions, with the deceptions of my art. Now, at length, I
have been caught in my own snare. That which I strove to enter
into and identify myself with, in order to win your approval and
applause, has entered into me, has made itself bone of my bone
and flesh of my flesh. It is not Ardalion the actor who now takes
leave of you. I am Ardalion no longer. I am a Christian. I confess

my faith in Christ, for I have seen the heavens opened and Him who was crucified standing on the right hand of God. You know what an ambitious man I have been, how I have never spared myself in the pursuit of my art. That ambition is now greater than ever, but its direction has changed. Now that I begin to be His disciple, I have no desire for anything visible or invisible, that I may attain to Jesus Christ. Let fire, let the cross, or the concourse of wild beasts, let cutting or tearing or torture unspeakable come upon me, so that I may attain to Him, my sole good and much-to-be-desired end."

After that, with arms outstretched, he prayed, giving thanks to Him by whose mercy he had been brought to this hour and made worthy to be numbered among His believing servants.

There is no need to describe the scene that followed. For a while the spectators, imagining the profession of faith to be part and parcel of the performance, broke out into tumultuous applause mingled with shouts of derisive laughter. When at length the plain truth of the matter dawned upon their astonished minds, a silence like that of death fell upon the assembly, a silence broken only when the real lictors arrived, to make an arrest that culminated in the trial and condemnation of the actor on the following day.

Ardalion suffered the extreme penalty in an open space in front of the theater that had been the scene of his many triumphs. Eyewitnesses without number testified that, as he walked to the place of execution, a mysterious brightness seemed to surround him, a radiance like that which falls from the sky at break of day. The noble profession of faith that he had been inspired to pronounce was never forgotten by the populace. He was subsequently accorded a formal notice in the Roman Martyrology, and his festival was kept on April 14. When, a few years after his death, peace

Christians Courageous

dawned on the stricken Church, many considered that the way had been smoothed for the reaction by the sacrifice of this player, for whom Christian truth had been lying in wait on the very road which seemed to be taking him forever out of its reach.

∞

The Blind Seer of Alexandria

The workshop of Aristemos, the silversmith, was frequented as much by the idle and the curious as by serious customers bent on doing business. For one thing, it was situated in the busiest quarter of Alexandria, and, being open to the street, it attracted attention as a matter of course. All day long, Aristemos would sit, tailor-wise, at his bench, only descending to attend to the charcoal furnace that was an essential part of his equipment. His products were famed for the delicacy of their workmanship — tiny figures in gold, silver, and bronze, carved and molded with exquisite artistry. Paradoxically enough, Aristemos attributed his success in this line to the fact that he was blind.

"It's your eyesight," he would say, "that gets in your way, and spoils your view, especially of small things"; and then he would add, with a smile, "Being able to see accounts for the blindness of most of us."

One evening, in the summer of the year 314, there came to the workshop a man whose demeanor suggested that an important transaction was in hand.

"Peace be to you, Aristemos!"

"Peace be to you!"

"Can you spare me some of your valuable time? The matter is of consequence."

"Most certainly! Let me put the shutters up, and then we shall not be disturbed."

When the workshop had been sealed off from the passersby, the two retired into a recess at the back, where the stranger came to the point without further ado.

"It is about my son Didymus. His twin brother was strong enough, but he was delicate from the start. He is now six years old, and eighteen months ago, fever brought him to death's door. By the mercy of God, he recovered, but at a terrible cost. He lost his sight."

"Ah," murmured the silversmith, "he is not the first in Egypt to encounter that misfortune, and he will not be the last. I often wonder why it is that there are more blind people in Egypt than anywhere else. But proceed!"

"I, his father, have employed the best physicians. I have taken him to Greece and to Italy. They could do nothing. For nearly two years now, no object of any kind has been able to pierce that terrible curtain that hangs in front of his beautiful young eyes — no object except the light of the Pharos. Darkness had fallen when we approached Alexandria on our return from Rome. For one ecstatic moment, I thought Didymus had recovered. He held his hands up in glee, as we neared the harbor, and kept repeating the word *fire*. But he was as blind as ever. It was not long before we found that out."

"Yes, yes. I also am able to discern the glare of the Pharos. Is it any wonder! Here is a beam rivaling the rays of the sun itself. They tell me that it is visible nearly thirty miles out to sea. Proceed! Proceed!"

"I have tried everything. I have made many distributions of alms in return for the potent prayers of God's poor; I have bespoken the penances and suffrages of the monks of our deserts. It has availed me nothing. Thrice has our patriarch, the Bishop Alexander, laid his hands upon those eyes. But it is not the will of God. *I am now resigned to that will. I come to you to know if you will help him.*"

"To be resigned?"

"Yes."

"But how?"

"He has made up his mind that he must learn about the things that are written in books. We, of course, know that it is impossible to educate one who is blind."

"Believe me, my friend, the day will come when that common opinion will be laid aside."

"You may be right. But, as I say, my son is all agog to learn, and now he insists on learning to *write*; that's his latest whim. I feel it my duty to satisfy those whims of his, and so help him to forget his terrible misfortune."

Aristemos nodded.

"Well," the other went on, "I will come to the point. Yesterday I heard by chance that, in some of the cities of Greece, the blind are taught to write by means of raised letters that they decipher by touch. They get to know the shape of the letters and the combinations of letters that form words; then, eventually, by practice, they are able to write the words down on paper. Have you ever heard of this invention?"

"Heard of it! I should think I have. I myself learnt to write by means of those very letters you speak of."

"But could you make me a quantity of such letters, in wood or even in metal? I can and will pay you handsomely."

After further discussion as to details, a bargain was struck there and then. Aristemos received fifty gold pieces on account, and contracted to supply as many letters, in the Greek orthography, as would suffice for the requirements of a young boy. The order was to be repeated, from time to time, as these requirements developed. The characters were to be done in bronze, on uniform counters one inch square. Metal slots of varying lengths were to be provided as well, and into these the letters could be fitted so as to form words. The work was to be ready in two months' time, and it would then be the duty of the tutors to familiarize Didymus with their shapes and names, and with the manipulation of the slots and counters.

The day soon came when the blind boy commenced the formidable task of committing to writing letters whose shape was revealed to him only through his sense of touch. His natural sagacity and his diligence were such that before long, he had made a beginning with the word *God*, following the custom of Christian children everywhere at that time. This he inscribed at the head of a parchment specially selected by his parents, the rest of the space being reserved for the Our Father. This he completed in due course, the lines being kept straight and parallel by means of a wire frame. It was a laborious and faltering effort, but the script was treasured in the family for generations. Great was the joy of his parents, and great was the joy of the silversmith Aristemos. It was felt that the lad now had an amusement sufficiently absorbing to divert his attention from the misfortune that had overtaken him. Little did they dream that this amusement, as they called it, was to be instrumental in turning Didymus into the greatest blind prodigy of all time.

As the months went by, the counters seemed to act upon the boy's system after the manner of a talisman. He was like a mountaineer: the further he advanced, the more did the horizon of possible exploration open up before him. By degrees, he became possessed by an ungovernable urge to know, to explore all the avenues leading to truth. He began to pay less attention to the counters and more and more to the tutors and professional readers provided for him. And, since speaking is far more exhausting than listening, it frequently fell out that these latter collapsed in their chairs and slept from sheer weariness. But the young lad, we are told, slept but little, either by day or by night; and, while he waited for his unconscious employees to come around, "he would chew the cud of what he had been listening to," as one of his earliest biographers puts it. This process, persisted in during his most pliable and impressionable years, resulted in a resounding victory gained over one of the heaviest forms of physical defeat.

Didymus acquired his knowledge with extraordinary rapidity. Before he was properly out of his teens, he knew nearly all that was to be known concerning the seven liberal arts of antiquity: Grammar, Rhetoric, Dialectics, Arithmetic, Geometry, Astronomy, and Music. At that date, these subjects were less restricted in their scope than now. Thus, Grammar embraced Philology and Literary Criticism, Geometry included Geography, and Music united the art of melody with that of poetic versification. The Bible Didymus knew almost by heart. He was well acquainted with the classical literature of Greece and Rome, which, in the fourth century, was accessible in all its undiminished abundance, or very nearly so.

∞

When he had just turned thirty, Didymus was placed at the head of the Catechetical School of his native city, the Christian Athens of this period. Over this religious university he presided as rector for half a century. His reputation spread through Christendom. He was renowned for his unworldliness, his deep piety, and for the gentleness and sweetness of his disposition. It seems, too, that he was endowed with what nowadays would be called psychic powers. He himself confided to a friend that the death in battle of the renegade and persecuting Emperor Julian, surnamed the Apostate, had been intimated to him while he slept in his chair. He saw white horses running to and fro, and heard their riders calling, "Tell Didymus that today, at the seventh hour, Julian died." Waking with a start, he made a note of the day and the hour, and before long the news came through that the emperor had perished exactly at the moment indicated.

In time, the erudition of this man became such that some of the foremost scholars of the day traveled long distances in order to consult him — St. Jerome, for instance, who spent a month in Alexandria, having certain obscure passages of Scripture explained by one whom he always referred to, not as "the blind" but as "the seer." He was visited also by one who, although illiterate, was yet a man of outstanding ability in his own line. This was Anthony, who, if he was not the first to lead the monastic life, was the first who ever attempted to lick it into shape. As might have been expected, he was inclined to make little of the loss of that which, to a contemplative, must be a constant source of distraction.

"I marvel," he said, "that a rational being can regret the absence of what, after all, he has in common with gnats and flies and ants. You should rather rejoice to find yourself in possession of that spiritual eyesight which you share with the saints and blessed apostles."

"Yes, but blindness is a heavy affliction for all that; so heavy that it was the special object of Christ's healing compassion. Imagine a plant being torn from its native soil! And this soil, adapted to give sustenance to all its roots and fibers, it must exchange for a patch of arid sand. Imagine a bird snatched from the light and freedom of the open air, and then caged in a dark cellar! Those who have their eyesight do not realize how strong our temptation is to let ourselves be engulfed in bitterness and repining."

"You, of course," said Anthony, "could remember a time when you were able to see. Perhaps that made the deprivation harder to bear."

"No, you are mistaken there. For a long time, my one comfort was the recollection of the sights I had seen: the cloudless sky over our city, the sun rising above the distant desert, the deep blue of the waters around our coast, the dazzling blaze of the Pharos on the edge of our harbor. The memory of these objects made me long for the night to come."

"Why so?"

"Because night brings sleep; and, in our dreams, we blind recover our sight. During the day, we live in a sort of tunnel through which we are trying to bore our way, as moles do through the earth of the fields — an endless tunnel it is, because the tiny rim of light that seems to lie at the end of it never comes nearer. But, in our dreams, we emerge from this tunnel, and we are rewarded for the privations of our waking hours. In these sightless visions, all objects, even the most ordinary, are decked out in unbelievable splendor."

"Sightless visions — ah! I have often wondered what the blind mean when they talk about seeing things."

"Well, I doubt very much if we could explain it even if we tried. Some have questioned the blindness of Homer, because in his poems he proves himself capable of shaping such striking images of natural objects like scenery, and so on. But we blind can form such images. There is no doubt about that. There is Phaleron, the musician, here in our city. All the world knows that he excels in his particular art. As you know, he is stone deaf. But he has told me, more than once, that he can hear his own compositions resounding in his head before ever they are played."

Then they fell to discussing the library for which Alexandria was famous even then, notwithstanding the heavy casualties it had suffered in recent centuries. Didymus had reverted to the subject of his early struggles, and to the sufferings he had endured, from the time he properly realized the magnitude of the disaster that had overtaken him.

"To be blind anywhere is hardship enough, but to be blind in Alexandria is the hardship of Tantalus, for it means that the treasures of the world's learning are forever near and, yet, forever out of reach."

That was how he put it.

It was true enough. In the year 332 BC, Alexander the Great had founded the city as a naval base. After his death, the government of Egypt was entrusted to the Ptolemies, who strove to make the capital one of the foremost cultural as well as commercial centers of the ancient world. Here learning, and particularly book-learning, was in the very air. The library soon became, and for long remained, the greatest collection of books to be found anywhere. Agents, armed with purses full of gold, were to be seen in the chief cities of Greece and Asia Minor, driving bargains with all and sundry who had manuscripts to sell. Meanwhile, advantage was taken of the city's outstanding importance as a trading center. Every ship entering the harbor was boarded by customs officers, and obliged to surrender all the manuscripts it happened to be carrying, whether they were part of the cargo or belonged to the passengers or crew. These were confiscated, and a receipt given for each. In an incredibly short space of time, an exact copy of each book would be made by the scribes and delivered up to the owners. The originals were placed in one or other of the two libraries.

After a good deal of persuasion, the government of Athens was induced to loan its official copies of the works of the three foremost Greek tragedians: Euripides, Aeschylus, and Sophocles. As a pledge of good faith, a deposit was exacted amounting to about

£5,000 of our money. Needless to say, the Alexandrines never returned the tragedies, and probably never intended to return them.
Money was no object to a people who could afford to spend
£248,000 on a lighthouse.

There came a time when this enthusiasm degenerated into the
mere ostentation, or vanity, of the bibliophile, anxious for the ad-
vancement not of culture but of his own prestige.

In the marshes of Lower Egypt flourished the papyrus reeds, out
of which many useful things were made, including the writing material we call paper. The emblem of this district was a tuft of papyrus, and it figures prominently on the monuments. The wide stalks
of this reed were stripped of their rind, and the pith beaten flat until it was very fine. After this, two layers were superimposed at
right angles and glued together. When dry, the finished article was
smooth and flexible, and ready for the pens of the scribes. These
were such expert calligraphists that, according to Pliny, the whole
of Homer's *Iliad* was written by one of them on a sheet that could
be folded up and put in a nutshell. When we talk about books, we
must bear in mind that the ancestor of the modern book is not the
clay tablet of the Babylonian, but the papyrus roll of the Egyptian.
The Greeks called papyrus *biblos*, from which they derived their
word for "book," and from which we derive our word for the
Scriptures.

Egypt, of course, exported large quantities of this handy writing
paper, especially to Greece and her colonies. One big customer
was Pergamum, whose library was for a time about as big as that of
Alexandria. Then some unpleasant Egyptian conceived the idea
of prohibiting the exportation of the papyrus plant, obviously
with a view to throwing the rival city into the shade. But the plan
miscarried, as it happened. Necessity is the mother of invention,
and the experts in Pergamum set to work to develop the process of

preparing the skins of animals for writing on. This experiment was so successful that the product became world-famous, and eventually supplanted the use of papyrus altogether. Parchment was much more expensive, certainly, but it did not perish so quickly or so easily as paper, it could be used on both sides, and it was possible to make erasions on it without destroying the surface.

Closely connected with the double library at Alexandria were workshops and offices, in which the business of transcribing, repairing, and cataloging was carried on night and day. In fact, the form and arrangement of modern books are largely derived from the skill and intelligence of the scholars and draftsmen in charge of this library, which, in its heyday, was reputed to contain no fewer than seven hundred thousand volumes. The books of that period, however, were real volumes; that is to say, rolled-up documents or scrolls; and these scrolls did not always contain a lot of reading matter. A work like the *Iliad* of Homer might account for as many as twenty rolls or volumes. We hear tell, however, of a single roll of papyrus being no less than 150 feet in length. When a sheet was ready for use, one end of it was inserted into a slit made in a cane. When the sheet was completely written on, a corresponding cane was usually attached to the other end, so that the volume could be rolled up either way. A tag was then affixed to one of the canes, giving a description of the book and the name of the author.

∞

"Yes," Didymus was saying, "we here in Egypt have always understood the importance of books, and the art and manner of making them. Do you know that, under the old idolatry, we had a God of Writing and a Goddess of Libraries? Thoth was the name of the former. He it was who, at the dictation of the supreme deity, inscribed on tablets a compendium of all possible knowledge. And when this same supreme deity destroyed the world with water, Thoth contrived to bury the tablets in the nick of time, and so saved knowledge from perishing from the earth."

"He was a kind of Noah," remarked Anthony.

"Exactly. And we Egyptians were not only the first to have collections of books to which all readers had access, but at a time when the rest of the world was illiterate, we were inculcating the reading of books as a religious duty. The main entrance of one of our early libraries had the inscription "The Dispensary of the Soul." I believe this was in the time of Ramses, the oppressor of the Hebrews. And at Memphis, the first of our capitals where the first of our kings lived, there was a factory in which skilled craftsmen were employed in copying and repairing books, and in manufacturing writing materials."

"And yet," Anthony interposed, "our Blessed Savior never applied Himself to the business of literary composition, or encouraged us to become authors or even readers. He Himself never wrote a line in His life."

"Pardon me," said Didymus, "you forget the lawyer who posed the question about the commandments. Him Christ told to seek the information he wanted in the pages of a book, the book of the Law. As for our Savior's own example, there is the eighth chapter of St. John's Gospel. According to that, He wrote twice, not indeed with any pen on paper or parchment, but with His finger in the dust of the temple courtyard. It may be that that was the manner of it, when human beings first took it into their heads to write at all."

"Yes," Anthony replied, "and with the next gust of wind that blew, the writing of our Savior was lost forever. Is there not a lesson there for you who devote your lives to the service of literature? Where are all these collections of books that you speak of? Many of them have disappeared already. Your own library here in Alexandria has been burned more than once, and may be again before long. Posterity may search, and search in vain, for a single copy of those treasures of learning which now fill the shelves you are so proud of."

"True," said Didymus, "that possibility has always to be reckoned with. I have known scholars who were inclined to regret our invention of paper because, for all their clumsiness, the old baked bricks and tablets and chiseled columns were at least guaranteed to wear well. And what you say about our Savior is discouraging enough certainly. As a corrective, let us remind ourselves that, although He never went in for writing, He was glad to avail Himself of the services of a library. In the synagogue at Nazareth, He borrowed the scroll of the prophet Isaiah and, having unwound it, He read and expounded it to the people. And He showed His respect for the volume by carefully rewinding it when He was finished, and giving it back, ready for the shelf, to the librarian."

Anthony laughed heartily at this, and allowed that he was no match for one skilled in the theory and practice of debate.

"I myself am no scholar," he admitted, "but I do not on that account despise learning, or think ill of those whose calling lies in that direction. Each one has his proper gift: let him use it to God's glory. I have been often asked how I have contrived to live for so long, in the wilderness, without the alleviation provided by books. My answer always is that nature is my library; on its ample shelves I have found all the instruction and diversion I have required."

"You, my Father," said Didymus, "have chosen the better part. You have become wise without books, whereas there are many of us who, though surrounded by them, remain half-witted and foolish."

The Blind Seer of Alexandria

∞

Again and again, by his contemporaries and by later ages, Didymus was acclaimed the world's most accomplished blind man, the one who more than any other exemplified the victorious element in human life — the heroism by which mind triumphs over matter, even the most intractable. However that may be, he is certainly not alone in this particular field of conquest, or anything like it.

Every century has produced, and no doubt will continue to produce, its blind prodigies. But what makes Didymus's achievement outstanding is the circumstance that he lived in an age when the education of the blind was looked upon as an impossibility. This error was not properly disposed of until 1784, when Valentin Haüy set himself to do for the blind what the Abbé de l'Épée had done for deaf mutes. Braille was a pupil in Haüy's school for the blind.

∞

Hide-And-Seek in Dead Earnest

Athanasius, Patriarch of Alexandria, was far and away the greatest leader the Christian body had to boast of in the fourth century. It was due to him, more than to any other, that that body was able to emerge, scorched but breathing, from one of the most trying ordeals in its long history. He may be said to epitomize, and even to personify, the crisis in question.

Naturalists tell us of certain marine birds that are at their best only in foul weather. When the hurricane blows its fiercest, then it is that, instead of cowering in the shelter of the land, they sally out to meet its onset and challenge its fury. Such, as its name implies, is the stormy petrel. Petrel is a diminutive of Peter, and the Peter referred to is the one who walked so fearlessly upon the Sea of Galilee. In the Bay of Biscay, when the billows are like inverted cataracts rising to enormous heights, these petrels can be seen in dozens carrying out their daring operations. One writer says of them that they are gifted with the proud prerogative of being afraid of nothing on earth.

Some human beings rather resemble these undaunted creatures. Athanasius was one of them. He was the stormy petrel of his day and generation. For more than half his long lifetime, he was compelled to do battle with powerful and numerous enemies. The enemies were so numerous, indeed, and to such an extent did the lion's share of the fighting devolve upon himself, that the contest passed into a proverb. Even now, after sixteen hundred years, any conflict of this kind, where the odds are overwhelming, is often described as another case of *Athanasius Against the World*. So great was he in every way that, as is usual with such people, a number of good stories grew up around his name and his fame. One of the best of them has to do with his boyhood years.

When he was quite a youngster — so the story goes — he and his companions were diverting themselves on the beach at Alexandria, just below the house in which the bishop, or patriarch, of that city resided. At that date, the question of converting the heathen was very much to the fore, particularly in this part of Africa. Alexandria was the missionary center of Christendom, and its catechetical school, besides being a training-ground for the apostolate, was a pattern to all other churches in its systematic preparation of candidates for Baptism. It was hardly surprising, then, that the game the lads were playing had to do with this very ceremony. One group of boys, representing the Gentiles, made themselves scarce among the sand-dunes, while the other group, led by a cross-bearer, went searching for them — a real hide-and-seek business. To Athanasius was allotted the most important role in the drama: the part of baptizer. As soon as a young "pagan" had been rounded up, he was promptly "arrested" and brought before the "bishop" to be baptized. The story goes on to tell how the real bishop was watching the game from the window of his study and how, when it was over, he sent for Athanasius, and placed him in the cathedral school to be trained for the priesthood.

Whatever may be the truth or otherwise of this tradition, what is certain is that, later on, Athanasius had to play the game of hide-and-seek for all he was worth, and as a matter of life and death. When he was only thirty years of age, he was put in charge of the church and the community which, tradition says, were founded by St. Mark, the man who wrote the second of the four Gospels. The Christian religion made rapid strides in this corner of the Dark Continent, thanks largely to the fact that two-thirds of the population of Alexandria were Jews. In the time of Athanasius, North Africa, including Egypt, was probably the most Christian portion of the ancient world.

The new bishop was small of stature; so small that his opponents made merry over it, the Emperor Julian describing him as a mannikin rather than a man. He had the lightly built, well-knit frame of the Egyptian, and this made him very nimble of foot and intensely energetic. He was remarkably quick-witted besides, with a sense of humor that never failed him, and a courage that never faltered even in the face of what looked like disaster.

He was going to need all these endowments, as it happened, because a struggle lay before him that was to last for nearly forty years. To be quick-witted and nimble of foot is an advantage to a man compelled to dodge and duck, and duck and dodge, for his freedom, if not for dear life, and do it at a moment's notice. Small things are always easier to hide than big ones, and that advantage also the mannikin had over the pursuivants and detectives employed to apprehend him.

The trouble was all the doing of a numerous and determined set of people called Arians, after their leader Arius, who was a priest working in Alexandria. The fourth century, which saw the end of the pagan persecutions, saw likewise the commencement of those serious quarrels which assaulted the Christian body from within; and no one of all the quarrels spread with greater violence or more sudden success than this one. Arius was by no means the sort of man who could be easily disposed of. He knew how to stick up for himself. He was prepared to fight for his own hand to the bitter end. Had he been a mere windbag or tub-thumper, he might have been left to blow or thump himself to a standstill. But he was nothing of the kind. His calm persuasive manner of arguing matched the simplicity of his life. He was good-looking besides, with something impressive, and even majestic, about his appearance; so much so, that the first of the thousands whom he succeeded in winning over to his ideas were some six or seven hundred nuns.

Arius, apparently, understood the business of propaganda and publicity. He threw his teaching into the form of a popular ballad, suitable for singing at banquets and merry-makings. This he distributed to all and sundry, including travelers and sailors, of whom large numbers were always to be found in and around the port of Alexandria. In this way, news of the dispute, and the dispute itself, spread far and wide. Before long, the entire Eastern world was agitated by the contest, and the ins-and-outs of Christian belief were being canvassed by the very pagans. Women squabbled about them at their house-doors, and rival gangs of children came to blows over them in the public streets.

In the finish, the conflict succeeded in splitting Christendom in two; and, when the split was at its widest, it was found that those on the left outnumbered those on the right by a formidable majority. And the worst of it was that the emperor himself openly sided with the Arians and, therefore, treated Athanasius as a traitor. Again and again he was banished; again and again efforts were made to have him apprehended and brought to trial. The hunted prelate had to conceal himself, at one time in a disused well, at another in the family tomb. He retreated, but he never surrendered; all his retreats were strategic ones. When open warfare became impracticable, he went underground. In fact, his is one of the first underground movements known to history. Before long, the elusiveness of this ecclesiastical Scarlet Pimpernel became a legend, and was talked about up and down the empire. To the bishop himself, it seemed, sometimes, as though he were destined to spend the greater part of his episcopal life either in exile or in hiding. Between the years 335 and 363, he was deposed from office six times. Things came to such a pass, in the end, that a price was actually set upon his head, and Alexandria itself could no longer guarantee him a place of asylum.

Fortunately, Athanasius could rely on the loyalty of the Egyptian monks, of whom, at that date, there were close upon a hundred thousand scattered along the Nile Valley. Many of the subordinate prelates whom he had consecrated were drawn from their ranks. There was one such, in particular, an Egyptian called Asar-Hapi, better known as Serapion. He was Bishop of Thmuis and, some years before, had gone to Rome to plead the cause of his persecuted superior. As soon as he had heard of the new danger that threatened, Serapion made his way to Alexandria by night and, in due course, was directed to the patriarch's hideout. He was accompanied by a couple of experienced monks, Petabast and Petarpometis by name, to whom the whole of the Nile Valley was as familiar as the palms of their own hands. They had much to say to one another, these two, but eventually they fell to discussing the present predicament, and to suggesting ways and means of getting out of it.

"No doubt," said the patriarch, "you have already heard how I come to be where I am."

"Not exactly," replied Serapion. "So far, we in Thmuis have had nothing to go by, except the version of the affair spread abroad by the Arians. And you know what kind of people they are."

"I do indeed," rejoined Athanasius. "These gentry are such good liars that you can hardly believe even the opposite of what they say. Twenty years ago, you remember, they accused me in open council of murdering the monk Arsenius, and of dismembering his body for purposes of magic. And when I produced the said Arsenius, and showed how alive and kicking he was for a corpse, they turned around and said I had restored him to life by magic. They are out to put me in the wrong, and they will do it by hook or by crook; that you may be sure of. But tell me, what do they say about the troubles of a month ago?"

"They say that you acted like a coward, and left your flock in the lurch in order to save your own skin. Of course, I took that with a big pinch of salt."

"It is just as well that you should know exactly what did happen, and I am going to tell you. When I was informed that I was no longer Patriarch of Alexandria and that a renegade had been elected in my place, my answer was that I would yield to nothing but force. Well, that very night, when our people were keeping vigil in the Church of St. Thomas, the governor of Egypt entered the city with a backing of over five thousand troops. They were well armed, too, some with swords and lances, some with darts and clubs. While we were singing away inside, they surrounded the building, posted guards at all the exits, and then broke in through the west door. From my chair in the chancel, I could see the soldiers beating about them with the flats of their swords, trying to make a gangway. But the people saw what they were at, and did everything to hinder them. I did not want anyone to be hurt on my account, so I told the deacon to intone the psalm *Confitemini Domino* — *Praise the Lord for He is good.* This he did, the congregation answering in its turn: *For His mercy endureth forever.* When this was ended, I stood up and commanded all who had taken part in the service to retire in good order and go home. The clergy wanted me to withdraw at this stage, but I refused to budge until the church was cleared. By this time, there was pandemonium, and a number of my people were trampled to death. Thereupon the clergy laid hands on me, and dragged me down from my place before the altar. And so, be truth my witness, though the soldiers blockaded the chancel and were in motion around the church, with the Lord leading me, I made my way through them and got out unperceived, feeling thankful that I had been enabled to see my flock to safety and, at the same time, to preserve my own life for a future occasion. I have sometimes regretted I am not a tall man, but I did not regret it at that time."

"And I," added Serapion, "I have sometimes regretted that bishops and clergy had no distinctive dress to mark them off from the laity. But you probably owed your life to the fact that you could not be recognized; you were just one man among hundreds, all wearing the same clothes."

"Yes, true enough."

"Well, then, that brings me to the purpose of my visit. You know perfectly well that you cannot remain here in the city any longer. They have offered big money for your capture, alive or dead, and such a reward is sure to prove too tempting to certain individuals. You must come with me to a place where you will be perfectly secure."

"To a place of hiding?"

"No. The best way to hide is not to hide at all. If you want to conceal yourself, go out into the open and mingle with the crowd. If I were a fugitive and my bald head were likely to give me away, my best plan would be to join a bald-headed community, and the bigger the community, the better. Do you see what I am driving at?"

"Yes, I do. You suggested it once before. You want me to go and live among your monks until the storm blows over. Well, this time I will take your advice. I remember when your Anthony came to see me, soon after my appointment, he told me that one day I would need the protection of the solitaries of the Egyptian deserts."

"You have been their consistent defender always, and anything they do for you now will be nothing but plain justice. Once among them, with this habit I have brought to cover you, you will be as difficult to identify as a particular straw in a whole bundle of straw."

"Perhaps so. But monasteries are easier to search than cities, and you know what has become of my latest attempts to hide in Alexandria."

"But in this case, a way of escape will always remain open to you. You will have the river at your back door, seven hundred miles of it, and mile linked to mile by means of the cells of our monks. You can be carried upstream, from one monastery to another, as far as the Thebaid and even farther. The soldiers will be reluctant to follow you as far as that. You know how terrified they are of the vengeance of Osiris, whose worship still lingers in that remote region."

Because there was something in this proposal that appealed to the boyish side of the patriarch's character, he consented without more ado. And thus it happened that, in the forenoon of the next day, the people thronging the main thoroughfare of Alexandria saw four men dressed in the threadbare garb of the monks making their way toward the Canopic Gate, heading, apparently, for the hermitages in the desert of Scete, which lay on the confines of Libya. They were doing no such thing, really, but they had chosen the hour and the point of their departure on purpose to create this impression. They followed the wild track leading westward until night fell, and then they turned about and directed their course to the southeast, leaving the monasteries of the Nitrian Valley on one side.

Fifteen days later they arrived at Memphis, where they were soon able to test the efficiency of the scout system to which Serapion attached so much importance. Within a week, news was brought to them, from Alexandria, that the soldiers of the governor were preparing to make a systematic search of the monastic settlements of Scete, in one or other of which they felt certain Athanasius had taken refuge on leaving the capital. Serapion could not conceal his satisfaction on receipt of this intelligence.

"They are doing exactly what I hoped they would do," he exclaimed. "They are walking into the trap we laid for them. I don't envy them their task. Scete is in the wildest part of the Libyan desert, fifteen days' march from Alexandria, in a place so inaccessible that even the monks themselves can reach it only by following the stars; which means that we shall not be disturbed for months, and can take it easy."

As it happened, this surmise proved to be correct. Taking their own time, the fugitive and his faithful escort now began a journey, by land and water, during which they moved, to and fro, in a perfect fairyland of historical monuments and memories.

Memphis, or Men-nofir, was Egypt's primitive capital, a city founded by Menes himself, the first of the host of kings who ruled over the Nile Valley. Here it was that the greatest of all the Pharaohs, Ramses II, set up those obelisks which are said to have cost the labor of twenty thousand men. The Egyptians appear to have specialized in the manufacture of these graceful tapering shafts of solid stone, often pink granite, with their points sheathed in bronze and their sides covered with inscriptions. They were cut and shaped according to a geometrical formula which varies hardly at all in each case.

In this neighborhood, too, Athanasius had a sight of the pyramids of Gizeh, the largest of which had been erected by Cheops some thirty-three centuries before. As far as we know, human hands have never constructed a bigger thing than this — the only one of the Seven Wonders of the World that has managed to survive. The mausoleum of Halicarnassus, the walls and hanging gardens of Babylon, the statue of Zeus at Olympia, the temple of Artemis at Ephesus, the Colossus at Rhodes, and the Pharos of Alexandria — all have disappeared, while the Great Pyramid still lifts up its pointed head to the sky. Nobody seems to know how the ancient builders contrived to move about the colossal pieces of masonry of which the pyramids are built, although there seems to be some grounds for believing that they cut them up by means of bronze saws, whose teeth were composed of precious stones. Everything about them was planned to secure a maximum of permanence, concealment, and security. Certainly their architects must be given full marks on all three counts. Fewer secrets have been better kept than theirs. In the fourth century, no one seems to have had any idea that these curious structures were really tombs.

In the vicinity of Memphis still lingered the legend of the beautiful Nitocris, the Egyptian queen mentioned by Herodotus, and the reputed original of the Cinderella story. One day — so the story goes — when she was bathing, an eagle swooped down, over the beach, and stole one of her gilded sandals. This it carried in its beak to the royal palace, and dropped in the lap of the reigning pharaoh. He was so fascinated by the charm of the tiny shoe that he searched the land, high and low, for the woman whose foot it fitted, and thereafter made her his queen.

Eventually the pressure of the chase drove the bishop upstream into the Thebaid, the province of Egypt of which Thebes was the capital. Thebes, or Uast, as the Egyptians called it, was the

antony lake

Hecatompylos of the Greeks, the City of the Hundred Gates. Here stood the huge Egyptian colossus, which the same Greeks took to calling the Statue of Memnon, and which, when the rays of the rising sun fell on it, gave forth a sound resembling that of a breaking chord.

Quite close to Thebes was Karnak, a perfect museum in itself. Conspicuous among its monuments is the royal shrine dedicated to Amen-Ra, with its Hall of Pillars built by the father of Ramses, some of whose columns are of enormous thickness and some sixty feet high. Later additions brought this temple to a total length of well over a thousand feet, surely one of the largest buildings ever erected. Across the plain of Thebes lay the Valleys of the Kings and Queens, containing the tombs of many of the most illustrious rulers of the country, together with their consorts. The discovery of these sepulchers by archeologists in 1879 was a major event for scholars, because it bridged the chasm separating the Ancient World from the New.

And so this memorable chase went on and on, until it looked as though the bishop would be driven across the southern frontier of the Empire at Syene, or Assuan. And all the time, he was as well guarded as the secret of the Egyptian tombs. The monks were everywhere, the main bodies mustering in great enclosures, but small parties continually traversing the highways, visiting the wells, the markets, the centers of population, the very billets of the soldiery.

They not only went everywhere, but they heard everything there was to hear, because they had relations and friends in every camp. In vain did the persecutors endeavor to elude the vigilance of these scouts; at the first whisper of their approach, the news would be carried from one monastery to another, right back to the bishop's headquarters for the time being. Then a mysterious boat would be run out, and pursuers and pursued would again lose contact the one with the other.

The monks of the Thebaid were cenobites; that is to say, groups of them were housed in what was called a cenobium. This was a typical Egyptian structure of tremendous solidity, with thick walls sloping inward and perforated by loopholes. These were the only windows, and they were situated at a great height from the ground. In some cases, the monks left and entered their habitation by means of one of these loopholes, to which a windlass was attached. Inside the walls, there were ample fields and gardens in which were cultivated the staple diet of the brethren: fruits and vegetables. These grew in great profusion: grapes, oranges, lemons, dates, melons, pomegranates, lentils, peas, beans, cabbages, cucumbers, leeks, onions, and garlic, not to mention wheat, barley, millet, and flax. The olive, too, was tended with great care, and we are told that forty flasks of oil went to the making of one salad.

Repeated searches were made for Athanasius in this neighborhood, but they were useless. He simply passed unperceived from one cenobium to another, until his exasperated persecutors had exhausted themselves. When things looked really dangerous, he took refuge in a cavern whose whereabouts was known to one person only, to his devoted companion Serapion, whose episcopal see of Thmuis was situated a little higher up the river.

And so at length this battle of wits came to an end after having lasted six years. The patriarch was restored to his church and people. But he never forgot those who had befriended him at such risk to themselves. It was to them that he dedicated his famous book about the Arians, a book he wrote while enjoying their hospitality.

Nor did he forget that other who had befriended him: the Nile. When threatened with assassination, during the reign of the Emperor Julian, he sought safety on its waters, and just in the nick of time. He had not gone far when he perceived that his boat was being followed by those entrusted with the execution of the crime. The patriarch appeared to be quite unconcerned. "Turn around," he said to the boatmen, "and let us go to meet these would-be murderers." It was not long before the hunters and their prey came face-to-face, the bishop, in the meantime, having muffled himself up in the monastic cloak he was wearing.

"Hi! You there! You monk! Have you heard or seen anything of the traitor Athanasius?"

"Yes," was Athanasius's reply. "He is quite close at hand. If you make haste, you will catch up with him."

The ruse was a complete success. Once again sheer presence of mind and calm assurance had won the day.

Blood and Sand

Nearly half a century had gone by since Telemachus exchanged the stir and bustle of his native city for the solitude of the Nitrian desert. For a time, and a long time, it had been a struggle; but by degrees the clamor of his human nature had died down until, at last, he was at peace.

At peace — except for one thing. On first coming into the wilderness, he had sought the advice of the great St. Anthony, the patriarch of monks, then over a hundred years old. The venerable man had confirmed him in his resolution.

"Go forward, my son": these were his words. "Let nothing turn you from your purpose. The time is coming when there will be demanded of you a sacrifice not unlike that of Calvary itself. It is only the desert that can nourish the heroism you will need when that great day dawns for you."

This was over forty years ago, and yet, so far, heaven had made no sign. "Has it forgotten me?" Telemachus would wonder sometimes. "Or is it that I am unworthy?" he would wonder again; and that second thought made him uneasy.

Meanwhile his days and nights were fully occupied, and not just with prayers and fastings either. For one thing, the group of cells that he and his fellow solitaries had built for themselves stood close to the delta and a league or so from the fifty-mile road running between the Sodium Lakes and the port of Alexandria. All the year round there was a come-and-go of traders and government officials traveling about their business. And, since from the earliest times, monks were pledged to the duty of exercising hospitality, the needs and necessities of these passersby involved a patient and continuous charity.

In those days, the behavior of the Nile affected people's health much as the behavior of the moon is said to affect some people in our time. When the water was rising or was due to rise, you were liable to become "river struck," and might have to lie by for days until your temperature went down. In nearly all the monastic settlements of Egypt, there was a special building set apart for casualties of this kind; the monks took turn about in looking after them. In this way, news of the outside world could hardly help reaching their ears. There was one item of information that gravely disturbed the conscience of Telemachus.

In the autumn of the year 399, a civil servant, whose name was Valerian and who was returning to Rome after a spell of duty, reported strange doings in that nominally converted capital. The old heathen worship had been more or less proscribed by Constantine's immediate successors, and Christianity was the acknowledged religion of the court. For all that, the Eternal City continued to be disgraced by one of the most revolting byproducts of paganism: those public shows, namely, in which men called gladiators fought and killed one another by way of providing amusement for the lookers-on. Telemachus himself had been born and bred in Constantinople, where such spectacles were unknown; and although he had heard of them, he had always thought of them as relics of an evil past, and relics that had been discarded. It was almost unbelievable that such crimes should be permitted to continue in a city consecrated by associations of the most sacred kind.

"But who are these people who do this, who kill one another for sport?" was his first question.

"They are of different kinds," was the reply. "They may be criminals who are going to die in any case, or they may be prisoners-of-war. When these are in short supply, they use slaves for the purpose. And these slaves and prisoners have no option in the matter. They are compelled to enter the arena; those who show the white feather are goaded on with red-hot bars. And, apart from these, there are the professionals, men who take the thing up of their own accord and who earn their living that way. These are trained in special schools subsidized by some of the rich senators. It is a regular business, you see. Those who have these professionals in their pay hire them out at so much a head and for so much a time."

"And Honorius, our most Christian emperor, allows it to go on?"

"He does indeed. But you who live in deserts do not realize that Rome is still a pagan city, just as the empire is still a pagan empire."

"But I thought that Constantine —"

"Oh yes; no doubt you thought that Constantine's baptism settled everything. But you are mistaken. He decreed the abolition of these gladiators and their murderous performances, just as his successors decreed the abolition of idolatry. But, my friend, sick people do not become well just because the physician writes out a prescription. Decrees or no decrees, the old shrines and statues are still to be seen everywhere. Why, at this very moment, the sacred fowls are being cared for and venerated; the ancient festivals are appearing in the calendar and are kept with the customary games. I myself have actually seen some of our own people turning to the east to salute the risen sun, and they on the point of entering the Basilica of St. Peter."

"But Honorius is not wanting in courage. Was it not by his order that the Sibylline Books were burned?"

"Yes, truly; and many of us regretted that burning, which posterity will doubtless regret even more. But it is one thing to consign a book to the flames, and quite another thing to eradicate instincts that have been in undisturbed possession of human nature for hundreds of years. My own feeling is that, even when the world has become really Christian, these ancestral instincts will yet contrive to reveal themselves somehow — reveal themselves by stealth, so to say, under cover of literature and art, and so on. You must understand that these bloody spectacles are of long standing. They say that they go back nearly seven hundred years, and originated in the human sacrifices formerly offered up in parts of Italy, especially at funerals."

"Hasn't the Church done something?"

"Yes; she has placed the profession under a ban, and no gladiator is allowed to be baptized until he has renounced the business."

"And yet the spectators are Christians?"

"For the most part, certainly. The blood-lust is too strong for them."

"And you! Have you ever patronized these shows?"

"I am ashamed to say that I have, Christian though I am. The first time I went for purely social reasons, just to put in an appearance. When the fighting began, I closed my eyes, resolved to see nothing. At last the uproar among the audience was so great that curiosity got the better of my resolution. I opened my eyes, and I kept them open. And, worse still, I returned again and again. I just could not stay away. You can't imagine the effect the thing has on you. Afterward, when your blood cools, you hate yourself for going. But the urge to return starts up, sooner or later. It is almost irresistible."

At this point, Valerian paused while a strange expression came into his face.

"I very much doubt," he resumed, "if the citizens will ever break with this abomination of their own accord. My own feeling is that there will have to be an intervention from outside."

"What sort of an intervention?" Telemachus asked.

"Well, I sometimes think that the Christ left the world too soon. There is so much still to be done, so many wrongs that have not yet been righted. You see what I mean."

"Yes, quite clearly. But, my friend, you forget about us; you and I, and the rest of us who bear His name, are His proxies, His nominees. Upon us it devolves to carry on where He left off. The kingdom He spoke of is a thing in the making, and we who believe in Him are called upon to complete what He left unfinished. Is it not written in our sacred Books that we have to supply what was wanting even to His sufferings?"

For a long time, there was silence between them, as though each was pondering the profound mystery of the Christian's vocation here below. The monk's gaze had wandered away from the face of his companion, away in the direction of his thoughts. For he was thinking now of an old man, clad in a rough cloak, and of certain words that had been uttered nearly fifty years before. "A sacrifice not unlike that of Calvary itself . . . the heroism you will need when the great day dawns for you."

On the last day but one of the same week, he and Valerian embarked at Alexandria on a corn-boat bound for Ostia. A fortnight later, they stood together before the main gate of the Flavian Amphitheater in the city of Rome. It was the first of January in the year 400.

Christians Courageous

∽

The Romans of the olden times were nothing if not good build-ers; they knew how to put materials together to form solid and durable structures. One of the most impressive monuments of their primitive skill is to be seen in the sewers of the capital, which were laid down as early as the sixth century BC. They inherited the Etruscan method of building an arch, and this they developed and completed by such inventions as the groined vault and the dome. They seem to have been the first to make an extensive use of bricks.

But of all the many fabrics produced by this practical people, the Coliseum ranks among the greatest. This is the name given to the theater erected in Rome some eighteen and a half centuries ago. A mighty receptacle capable (according to a contemporary document) of swallowing eighty-seven thousand spectators at one gulp, it was the joint effort of three emperors, each of whom be-longed to the Flavian family; hence, the name: the Flavian Am-phitheater. The Romans may have built bigger things than this, but this is the biggest thing of theirs in the shape of a ruin that has managed to survive.

That it ever became a ruin at all was due to a succession of un-fortunate circumstances. A big portion of the shell collapsed in the earthquake of 1349. During the next four centuries, this enor-mous mass of fallen stone served as a quarry, providing materials for at least four churches as well as other public buildings. In the fifteenth century, one contractor made off with 2,500 cartloads and, a century later, Cardinal Farnese, having obtained permis-sion from his uncle Pope Paul III to take as much stone as he could remove in twelve hours, mustered four thousand men on the day appointed. This sort of vandalism roused public opinion, and an end was at last put to the process of spoliation. Today, enough of the Coliseum remains to let us see how majestic-looking it must have been when it was new and whole.

More important than good looks, this building admirably fulfilled its architectural purpose, which was to provide the largest possible audience with the clearest possible view of the performance. Shaped like an ellipse, 1,790 feet in circumference, 620 feet long and 525 feet wide, its seating accommodation rose in concentric rows to a height of nearly 160 feet, and in such a way that no obstruction of any kind interposed between the onlookers and the spectacle going forward in the arena. Obviously it was not possible to put a roof on a building of such a size, since that must have necessitated the use of pillars. But the spectators could be sheltered from the sun by means of awnings supported on masts made of pine. These masts rested on corbels — that is to say, on stone supports projecting from the main wall, and built around to form sockets. Certain "reconstructions" of the Coliseum convey the impression that this fabric was made of silk, and was in one piece — a kind of spider's web production with an aperture in the center. This would mean something record-breaking in the shape of embroidery; something bigger than the Bayeux Tapestry, which is seventy yards long and, therefore, far bigger than the Veil of the Temple, which is said to have measured as many feet, and to have had a thousand figures of angels woven into it. We may omit Solomon's Carpet, which was supposed to provide standing-room for his entire army; that matchless textile seems to have issued from the looms of some poet's imagination.

If disgrace attaches even to the ruins of the Coliseum, this arises from the ignoble uses to which that superb building was put. Begun in the year 72, and dedicated by Vespasian seven years later, its immediate purpose was to provide the Roman populace with large-scale opportunities of diverting themselves with spectacles of cruelty and bloodshed. Every corner of the earth was searched to provide strange beasts — hippopotami, crocodiles, and white elephants. In Africa it was forbidden by law to kill a lion, even in self-defense, so necessary was it that the Romans' thirst for slaughter should be fully satisfied. In the time of Pompey, six hundred of these animals were killed in one day. Then the human performers took to killing one another. During the games organized by Trajan, which lasted for 120 days, ten thousand gladiators were slain, as well as the same number of animals. In the end, these homicidal exhibitions became part of the social and political life of Rome, and leading men staged them with a view to catching votes and maintaining their ascendancy. Latterly, the gladiator was generally a member of those races who were destined to destroy Rome and exact a terrible retribution upon the city of blood. Sometimes the arena would be flooded to furnish the sensation of a real naval battle.

∞

As the posters on the walls indicated, the performance that Telemachus and his desert acquaintance were waiting to see had already been running for ten days. It was being subsidized by Stilicho, the reigning emperor's father-in-law and the commander-in-chief of his army. The monk was horrified by these placards, which calmly announced the different kinds of combats about to take place and the numbers of fighters participating in each.

Presently the gates were unbarred and thrown wide open, and the enormous crowds lined up before them disappeared as though sucked in by a whirlpool. Thanks to the flights of stone steps ranged all around the building, and the doors giving access to the tiers of seats, the Coliseum could be filled about as quickly and as smoothly as a modern football ground. Valerian and Telemachus had not far to climb. Reaching the first landing, about ten feet from the ground level, they passed under a small archway and found themselves on the very edge of a low wall surmounted by a railing. This enclosure divided the spectators from the arena and was designed to protect the former from the fury of the maddened animals and subhuman contestants. As an additional security, armed guards patrolled the passageway between this wall and the *podium*, or marble terrace, on which were situated the best seats in the building. These were reserved for the senators and government officials. Valerian was entitled to a place here; Telemachus, who had taken care to cover his monk's habit with a white cloak, passed for one of his associates.

In an incredibly short space of time, the auditorium was filled to capacity; and, when the members of the orchestra filed into place, the din of voices died down to a whisper. Almost immediately, a latticed iron gateway, resembling a portcullis, at the base of the protecting wall, was drawn up, and the gladiators emerged and, with military precision, made the circuit of the arena. This diversion was followed by the formal test of the weapons, carried out by a stage-manager deputed to this office by the editor, or producer, of the show. When the gladiators had loosened their muscles and joints by means of a mock skirmish, with wooden swords and spears, a trumpet sounded and the serious business of the evening began.

To the inexperienced eye of Telemachus, the first pair to engage seemed to be very ill-matched. On the one side, there was a soldierly-looking individual, helmeted and armed with a shield and short sword, while his puny, meanly clad adversary had a long unwieldy trident, or three-pronged spear, in his right hand, and in his left carried what looked like a small fishing-net. The purpose of this net Telemachus was soon enabled to see. For a while it looked as though the fight could end in only one way. But what the second man lacked in strength, he made up for by his nimbleness; and this gave him an easy victory. He ducked and dodged with amazing agility, and when his chance came, he cast his net with such skill that his opponent was fairly entangled. Then, with one thrust of his trident, he brought him to the ground severely wounded. The net-carrier then stepped back a few paces, while the injured man exercised his right of appeal for mercy. This he did by raising his right arm and forefinger, whereupon a waving of handkerchiefs among the spectators gave the signal that his life was to be spared.

And so it went on. The pairs succeeded one another in rapid succession, some of them bearing nothing but clubs, others heavily armed with swords. They fought on horseback and they fought from chariots. Cruelest thing of all, they fought with their heads encased in helmets that had no eyepieces, so that they were hacking at, without being able to see, one another. The clemency shown in the first combat was seldom repeated. Instead of handkerchiefs, the spectators flourished their clenched fists or inverted thumbs, which meant that the prostrate fighters were slaughtered where they lay, their bodies being carried out on stretchers by the attendants. The pairs gave way to groups that engaged one another in battle formation, until the sand of the arena was dyed with blood and the air filled with the cries of the dying men.

And the strange thing was that, as far as Telemachus could see, no one viewed these butcheries with any appearance of disgust. Valerian had been right. Afterward, no doubt, when the thing was reviewed in cold blood, there would be a reaction. But for the time being, reaction there was none; not so much as a muttered protest or a gesture of disapproval. The voice of pity, if anywhere there was such a voice, was drowned in a tumult of frenzied shouts and yells; and, all the time, the attendants moved calmly from tier to tier, dispensing those Syrian perfumes used to keep down the stench of the blood.

Then, with startling abruptness, the thing happened.

To Valerian's astonishment, his companion arose, threw off the cloak covering his habit, clambered over the rail and dropped heavily to the floor of the arena. He was on his feet in a moment, however, and before he could be checked, had crossed over and placed himself between the combatants. A murmur ran through the vast audience. Even the gladiators themselves gave over fighting, and stood motionless, waiting to see what this madman intended to do.

What he did was a simple thing enough. Brandishing a wooden cross which he carried in his belt, he held it up at arm's length. Then, in a voice that could be heard from end to end of the vast building, he called upon the populace to make an end, once and for all, of a custom that was bringing disgrace upon the good fame of their city and emperor alike. "I demand it," he said, "not in my own name, but in His name who shed His blood in order that we might not wantonly shed the blood of another."

A deathlike silence followed this appeal, and the faces of the spectators plainly revealed the deep impression it had made upon them. But there was one at least who did not share the general feeling. Perhaps Alypius, the Prefect of Rome, had little use for monks; perhaps he resented what he chose to regard as a treasonable slur upon his master the emperor. Standing up and signaling to the performers, he bade them do their duty. "Do your duty; he deserves to die." The gladiators needed no further encouragement, and Telemachus was struck down, pierced, like Caesar, by twenty mortal wounds.

Blood and Sand

The Coliseum remains to this day, and the yawning gap to be seen in its walls symbolizes the breach made in a criminal custom of centuries' duration by the sacrifice of an old man who happened to be a hero. This monk's blood was needed to seal the abolition of those games of blood; it was, in fact, the last shed in an arena over whose sand so much had flowed. Telemachus had no sooner fallen than public opinion began to react violently against the abuse that had prompted his protest and occasioned his tragic death. The clamor of the populace forced the irresolution of Honorius, so that an edict of that same year proscribed the gladiatorial shows forever. In our time, that ancient amphitheater exhibits only signs of peace: plants growing among the stonework, birds building nests, and, in the center, a plain representation of the Christian cross.

∞

The Scourge of God

By way of distinguishing those speaking a different language from
them, the ancient Greeks coined the word *barbarians*. Such people
were babblers, human beings whose speech sounded more like *bar-
bar, bar-bar* than anything else. When the Romans came to the
fore, they adopted the title and applied it first of all to those outside
the pale of their civilization; and later on, to the tribes and races
living on their borders who, in the middle of the second century,
began to menace the peace and even the security of the empire.
The cultured West had been accustomed to laugh at these uncouth
warriors, but there was very little laughing done after 378, when
the Goths defeated and killed the Emperor Valens at the battle of
Adrianople. Here, mailed cavalry appeared in warfare for the first
time — the beginning of a fashion destined to last for a thousand
years.

Eventually it was not one inundation that had to be coped with
but a round dozen and more. Huns, Goths, Franks, Vandals — to
mention only some of the aggressors — were crossing the frontiers
at every point. They came down the Valley of the Danube, and
thus made themselves masters of the roads leading to the Balkans
and beyond; they reached the passes of the Alps and menaced

Italy. The Rhine, the Vosges, the Cevennes, the Pyrenees — these formidable barriers were of no avail, as Gaul and Spain soon knew, to their cost. They crossed the North Sea and occupied Britain; they crossed the Mediterranean and occupied North Africa. They swooped down from the heights of the Caucasus and spread over the Middle East. As a contemporary, with a taste for the picturesque, put it, "The Wolves of the North, after having devoured everything, came to drink in the waters of the Euphrates."

By about the middle of the fifth century, the terror heretofore distributed among so many objectives was concentrated on one single man, and a stunted, almost deformed man at that. Of all the leaders of the barbarian hordes, the most disappointing in appearance, and the most dreaded, was Attila, the king of the Huns. These Mongols from the Far East had crossed the Volga about a hundred years before and were, in Attila's time, firmly established in the territory now known as Hungary. Having conquered many of the German and Slavonic nations, he was able to rally them to his side and lay waste the provinces of the empire south of the Danube. His progress in this direction was checked by means of a tribute amounting to two thousand pounds' weight of gold.

Thanks to this heavy bribe, the Huns were kept out of sight as far as Italy and Rome were concerned. But a retired Greek soldier named Ammianus Marcellinus happened to publish a history of Rome about this time, and the contents of this work, which was written in Latin, filled the West with consternation. According to this contemporary authority, Attila's people were more savage than any race of mortals hitherto discovered. With their stumpy limbs, overgrown heads, and unwieldy bodies, they were more like two-legged beasts than human beings. All the known endurance tests they could pass with flying colors: heat, cold, hunger, thirst, and fatigue. They considered it effeminate to dwell in anything that had a roof on it; consequently, on the rare occasions when they settled down, they used their open wagons as houses. But normally they lived on horseback; they ate and drank, bought and sold, conducted the affairs of their nation, and even slept in the saddle. They plundered in order to exist, and existed in order to plunder; and, when they made a raid upon a strange territory, they descended upon their booty like a whirlwind coming down from the mountains.

Sure enough, in the early part of the year 451, Attila's standard moved toward the West. After a march of 800 miles, the Huns and their allies crossed the Rhine on a bridge of boats and, having sacked the chief cities of Belgic Gaul, advanced to the walls of the great metropolis called Aureliani (Orleans) after the emperor who founded it. Here, owing to the energy of its bishop, Anianus, his progress was halted long enough to enable the combined forces of the Romans and the Goths to assemble and march against him.

The result was that one of what are claimed to be the Fifteen Decisive Battles of the World was fought in the Catalaunian Fields, a level plain situated, roughly speaking, between Verdun and Châlons-sur-Marne, in that district of France famous for its champagne. The site of Attila's camp is visible to this day, in the shape of a series of grassy hillocks and deep ditches, obviously the remains of the earthworks and trenches his sappers had hastily made to protect his baggage as well as the weak spots in his defenses. The force he threw into the fray is said to have numbered seven hundred thousand men, drawn from the thirty nations he had already subdued.

During one long midsummer's day, the tide of conflict ebbed and flowed with varying fortunes on both sides. Three hundred thousand of the combatants lost their lives, so that for many a day, the peasants of the district were able to stake their vines with the bones of the slain, just as had been done, four and a half centuries before, when Marius defeated the Teutones at the battle of Aix. When darkness put an end to the fighting, the Huns were, apparently, as much masters of the field as their opponents. But in his secret soul, Attila knew that this last expiring effort of the ancient Roman valor had been too much for him; and that, should the combat be renewed on the morrow, disaster was almost inevitable. Too proud to fly, too proud to surrender, he ordered the horses to be stripped of their wooden saddles. With these, he caused to be erected in the center of the camp an immense funeral pyre, upon whose upper platform he assembled his war-chest, his chiefs, and the members of his family. Then, after giving instructions that the pyre was to be lighted in the event of the enemy breaking through the outer palisade, he climbed to the top, and sat down upon his throne to await the good pleasure of the coming morning.

But the battle of Châlons was over. Attila was not molested. He and the remnants of his army were allowed to depart in peace. Within a week, he was back again on the far side of the Rhine; within a fortnight, he had recrossed the Danube.

For twelve months, the monarch nursed his humiliation and his revenge. Then, on a sudden, he appeared at the head of the Adriatic and proceeded to besiege Aquileia, the key to Italy. In spite of a formidable array of battering rams, movable turrets and engines that could throw darts, stones, and even fire, this strategic city held out for three months. By all accounts, it very nearly escaped altogether. According to the records, Attila was on the point of giving up the struggle when he happened to see a stork forsaking the nest it had built on the roof of one of the houses. From this circumstance the wily Hun drew the same conclusion that sailors draw when they see rats deserting certain ships. Instead of retreating, he ordered the assault to be intensified, especially at that part of the battlements near which the nest was situated.

As a reprisal for its tenacity, this strongest of all the maritime cities of the Adriatic was leveled to the ground, after which Attila proceeded to ravage the rich plains of Lombardy. Then he rested his troops in the vicinity of Mantua, and prepared for his march on Rome, the object of his most extravagant dreams.

∞

Meanwhile, down in the threatened capital, the competent authorities were by no means disposed to try conclusions with an enemy safely entrenched behind the largest river in Italy. Of the senators no man spoke with greater knowledge than a certain Priscus who, four years previously, had been sent on a goodwill mission to the court of Attila. Shrewd and observant, he had made a careful study of the Huns and of their leader; and now, in the early summer of this fateful year, he sat before the door of his villa, discussing the situation with his colleague Maximus.

"The Consul," Priscus was saying, "dare not risk another battle, bereft as he is of the assistance of his Gothic allies."

"But, surely, they will rally to his banner if called upon."

"I am not so sure. In any case, it is a downright dangerous thing to bring these Goths into Italy, even as confederates. The mere sight of our land goes to their heads like wine, and makes them drunk with covetousness. No, no, Aetius [the Consul] knows what he is about. At the moment, he is the sole guardian of the public safety, and he is guarding it all right."

"Personally," said Maximus after a pause, "I think that Rome's day is over, and that we must reconcile ourselves to seeing her going the way of all her mighty predecessors: Egypt, Assyria, and Greece."

"How can you be so pessimistic?"

"Well, I am still pagan enough at heart to credit the ancient auguries. According to these, the empire has now reached the appointed term of its existence and must get ready to die. Everybody knows that Romulus, the founder of Rome, by slaying his twin brother, purchased from the fates a lease-of-life for the city stipulated at twelve centuries. Since Rome was founded 753 years before the coming of Christ, it is evident that the lease is on the point of running out. And now here comes this Attila. Everybody knows that he and his twin brother, Bleda, founded the city of Buda there on the bank of the Danube. And everybody knows that, while that city was building, Attila slew his brother, just as Romulus did; and by that blood-offering, he secured for his capital, and for his dynasty, the lease-of-life that Rome is about to forfeit."

"As for me," replied Priscus with a laugh, "I have long ceased to attach importance to these childish fables. I do not despair of Rome even now. And I do not despair of the future. My dabbling in philosophy has taught me one thing at least: that every prosperous and productive period of history is inaugurated amid ruin and disaster. Let us not judge the future by the present. Today, I grant you, we can see hardly anything but violence, destruction, and bloodshed. But tomorrow may well be quite different; and, of course, I speak of a tomorrow anything up to a couple of hundred years from now. I cannot help thinking that these savage hordes are the instruments of providence, as far as our part of the world is concerned. My belief is that the West shall absorb them all, Christianize them all; in short, that they are the nucleus of an empire greater than Cesar ever planned — a different kind of empire."

"In the meantime, what about our mutual friend Attila?"

"Like all Asiatics," Priscus went on, "Attila is a firm believer in omens and portents, and it is along that line that our deliverance will come. Dwarf of a man though he be, he really believes himself to be, what he always says he is, the instrument of Divine Justice. He grew up with that big head of his full of such fancies. He actually claims that the sword he carries is the identical one the Scythians of olden time worshiped as a god. Their oracles maintained that it disappeared from the earth long ago, and would not return until a warrior arose who was worthy to receive it. Attila claims to be that warrior, and to be in possession of that miraculous weapon which, he says, was found embedded in a field near his residence, and was identified by his wise men as being the Sword of Tyr [Thor's younger brother]. But, dear me! There is no end to the number of these magic swords, embedded in the ground and waiting for the chosen ones to draw them out."

Priscus was certainly right there. The myths of the past furnish quite a list of such weapons. Arthur's one, Excalibur, was found stuck fast in an anvil, in the great church of London, with the inscription: "He who can draw this forth, the same is to be king."

"Up to now," Priscus continued, "Attila has been willing to swallow whole all that his flatterers have chosen to tell him. Since last year's battle, however, he has been indulging in a good deal of incredulity. His soldiers were brought up to believe that he could always make the rain and the wind fight in his favor. Yet not a drop of rain fell that day, and there was not breeze enough to stir the plumes of the warriors' helmets. They gave out that, as long as he wielded the Sword of Tyr, he would be able to scatter his enemies like chaff. Our legions have pricked that bubble. People are now saying that Attila turned tail after the fight, because he was intimidated by the story that went the round of his camp."

"What story?"

"It was to the effect that there were two battles fought that day, one on the ground and the other in the air. The soldiers said that they could see the ghosts of the slain, horses and all, charging one another in the summer haze hundreds of feet above the plain. We must take advantage of the man's peculiar mentality. In his own crude way, he worships the divine will. Let him be once persuaded that that will decrees that he spare Rome, and our troubles will be over."

"But who is to do the persuading?"

"Who, indeed, but Leo the venerable bishop of our city."

"Do you seriously suppose," asked Maximus, "that this Scourge of God is going to take orders from an unarmed man, is going to spare Italy after having ravaged Thrace, Illyricum, Macedonia, Moesia, Achaia, Greece, Pannonia, and Germany? Is it likely that one who exercises undisputed control over every foot of ground between the Caspian and the Rhine will renounce the conquest of a city such as Rome, and all at the bidding of an old man with nothing in his hand but a cross?"

"I say that it is worth trying. These barbarians are unaccount-able people. They were on the point of sacking Toulouse when Bishop Exuperius appeared on the walls in his robes and stopped them. Alaric spared the lives of all who sought refuge in the churches. Look what happened four years since in the ancient stronghold of the Parisii. When Childeric, the king of the Franks, took the city, he spared the lives of the prisoners at the bidding of Genevieve, all because she was a religious woman. Attila himself stood in awe of that same Genevieve, as he did of the Bishop of Orleans. Bishop Lupus saved the city of Troyes from destruction simply by going out, unarmed and unattended, and demanding an interview with Attila himself."

Leo, the Bishop of Rome referred to, was a man of learning and integrity above the usual. He shares the title of "the Great" with only one other pope out of the 260 who have so far held that posi-tion. Before many days, he who was ready to encounter any danger in defense of his flock was hastening northward, accompanied by the Consul and many of the senators, in order to reason with "the wearer of the twelve crowns." The deputation found the Huns encamped at the confluence of the Mincio and the Po, not far from the place where the poets Virgil and Catullus had their farms. In due course, an audience was arranged at which the pontiff spoke somewhat after this fashion:

> We who stand here, O King of Kings, represent the Senate and the People of Rome who, from being the conquerors of the universe, now appear before you as vanquished suppliants. Surely such a state of affairs must satisfy the ambition even of the most ambitious. With the Mistress of Mankind prostrate at your feet, nothing is now wanting to your glory, save the crowning merit of sparing the vanquished, and respecting what is no longer capable of defending itself. To destroy Rome can add nothing to such fame as yours. On the contrary, it must detract from it. Should that first city of the world become the prey of spoliation, posterity will execrate as evil counselors those who urged Attila to a deed as wanton in the sight of men as it is impious in the sight of God.

While these words were being spoken, the monarch stood to attention, with his eyes fixed upon the face and features of him who dared to utter them. And, lo and behold, all of a sudden, there appeared the apostles Peter and Paul, dressed like bishops, standing on the right and left of Leo. They were brandishing swords, and seemed to be threatening Attila with death if he did not hearken to the Pope's entreaty. On this, he who had heretofore raged to and fro like a madman, promised a lasting peace and withdrew beyond the Danube.

As to the future of the West, the forecast made by Priscus was verified to the letter. Within a year, Attila was no more. With his passing, the fabric of his conquests fell to pieces; and, before long, the total disappearance of the Huns, who had started all the trouble, was to provide history with one of its major conundrums. The barbarian invaders were subdued at last, not by force of arms so much as by the logic of events. The old civilization did not quite succumb to their savage assaults, nor did Caesar's empire become a Mongolian desert. Out of the welter of those alien tribes and races emerged the Christendom of the Middle Ages, and that distinctive type of human being recognizable the world over: the European.

∞

The Man from the Sea

More than one sea voyage has left a mystery behind it, beginning with that of Jason, and his fellow heroes, who went sailing in the good ship *Argo* to carry off the Golden Fleece. This expedition took place not long after the Trojan War — that is to say, over three thousand years ago. Yet, there is still discussion among the experts as to the route it followed, at any rate on its return.

Until such time as our planet had been properly surveyed and charted, it was easy for the mariners themselves to be mystified about the identity of the strange lands they visited. It was not until the fifteenth century that seafarers began to be provided with maps that could be called serviceable maps. These were of Italian origin, and they did make some attempt to be accurate about such things as coastlines and headlands.

But even so, these maps were rough and ready, and could easily lead the sailors astray. We know that many vessels of the Spanish Armada were wrecked off the Scottish and Irish coasts. One theory is that they were lured to destruction by their own maps, which were content to show the outline of the mainland, with never a hint of the reefs and islands strewn so plentifully in these western waters.

And, of course, the maps in question did not show the New World at all. Everything in that direction was conjectural and mysterious. Indeed, mystery had surrounded that part of the globe from the earliest times. Here was situated the Lost Atlantis — that island, as large as North Africa and Asia Minor put together, which in one terrible night of destruction sank beneath the waves, never to be seen again. This unique physical upheaval, if it ever really occurred at all, was brought about by the behavior of some wandering planet that caused a sudden tide-bulge around the earth. This tide-bulge produced a flood colossal enough to sink a whole continent. Such, at least, is the theory.

In a book published as late as 1154, the Atlantic is called the Sea of Darkness, because "no one knows what exists beyond it, and because the way to it is barred by storms and sea-monsters." This darkness was not dispelled until several centuries later, so that sailors continued to be very chary of venturing into it. Europeans got as far south as the Cape Verde Islands, in the middle of the fifteenth century, but they hesitated to go farther, because they had been taught to believe that no white man could sail much farther without being turned black.

This general mystification accounts, in part, for the difficulty we have in determining who first discovered America. It may have been the Italian after whom that continent is named. A year before Columbus made his landing, Amerigo Vespucci sailed westward from the Canaries and, after twenty-seven days, came upon a coast he thought to be a continent. It may have been the continent of America, although Amerigo never actually claimed that it was. He just did not know. About five hundred years before that, a Norwegian ship sailed from Greenland and made settlements in places that were later supposed to be situated on the American coast. But the explorers themselves never knew where they were.

And, after all, even Columbus himself discovered America by mistake, so to say. He was really trying to find a westerly sea route to India, and he thought that Haiti, the island he had landed on and which he named Española, was situated in the Indian seas. This error was not dispelled until Balboa crossed the Isthmus of Panama twenty-one years later, and found, not India, but the Pacific Ocean.

Among the classical voyages that have left the world guessing must be ranked the one made in the sixth century by the monk Brendan, surnamed, and very rightly, "the Navigator." Prince Henry of Portugal is also known to history as "the Navigator." But, strictly speaking, his is only a courtesy title. Henry never accompanied the voyages he planned. He built a sort of Whitehall on the Portuguese coast, near Cape St. Vincent, where Admiral Jervis gained his victory, and here he studied all the matters connected with seafaring. He had shipyards in which, under his direction, three-masters competent to make long voyages were built. There, however, Henry's navigational operations ended.

But Brendan not only organized the famous expedition associated with his name; he captained it as well, and so wisely that he brought his ship safely back to port after a voyage lasting seven years.

This romantic individual, who is one of the patron saints of sailors, was born in the neighborhood of Tralee. In that rugged district he has left behind several memorials. There is Brandon Bay and Brandon Head; and there is Brandon Hill, the second-highest mountain in Ireland, rising to three thousand feet and commanding one of the finest sea-views obtainable anywhere. Due west is the North Atlantic, some three thousand miles of unbroken ocean reaching to the coast of Labrador. If you look over your right shoulder, there is water again as far as the mouth of the Shannon, forty miles away. To the left, you have Dingle Bay, with the

Christians Courageous

Blaskets lying at its entrance, one of the outposts of the European continent.

As to his motive in setting sail in the first instance, we have a choice of conjectures. Knowing what kind of man Brendan was, we might reasonably infer that he was looking for new lands to annex to the Faith of Christ. His was the Golden Age of Irish missionary activity, a period during which the sails of the Celtic monks were to be seen on all the northern seas, from Iceland to the mouth of the Somme. On the other hand, Adamnan, the author of the first *Life* of St. Columba, tells us that these monastic rovers were impelled by an irresistible longing for the quintessence of solitude; they were searching for some remote island or other, some fastness in the waste of the ocean, where no one could disturb them, and from which they could never be brought back.

It is not unlikely that Brendan was animated by that natural love of adventure which sends people on strange and dangerous quests, even in our time, when such quests tend to become scarcer and scarcer. There is plenty of evidence to show that these seafaring monks loved the sea for its own sake. The Irish monasteries of the date produced a class of literature unique in the annals of the cloister; the *Imramha* they are called — that is to say, books or writings concerning sea expeditions. A monk who was a countryman and contemporary of Brendan's, Columban by name, left behind a boat song of eight stanzas, a kind of sea-shanty; and men do not make a song about the things they have no love for. We have, besides, a scholarly geographical survey written, at the beginning of the ninth century, by an Irishman called Dicuil, who tells us that, for much of his information, he was indebted to the firsthand knowledge of the Irish sailor-monks.

And sure enough, we are informed, on good authority, that Brendan never tired of climbing the hill called after him and, from its top, studying the sea-view in all its varying moods and tenses: at dawn, when the glory of the morning was diffused over its wide reaches; at midnight, when the stars swept around the pole; and more especially, at eventide, when the setting sun opened up a pathway of burnished gold leading to the unknown beyond. Every distant prospect has something enticing about it. We long to come to close quarters with the objects of our contemplation; if they are hills, we want to climb them; if they are valleys, we are impatient to explore them. Maybe, then, it was this enticement that sent Brendan sailing away westward, one of a crew of eighteen, on a quest lasting for seven years.

If we are to go by legends, there is one of these to the effect that what he went off to look for was nothing more nor less than the Islands of the Blessed, that paradise of the ancients into which the sorrows of earth never enter, and where peace and beauty forever dwell. The existence of these mysterious islands was rooted in a tradition that had drifted down from early times, when the poets of Greece located them somewhere in these very seas. Homer's Elysium was a meadow on the bank of the river Oceanus which flowed beyond the Pillars of Hercules. But Pindar pictured it as a group of islands:

> 'Round these the Ocean breezes blow,
> And golden flowers are growing.

So far, the poets. The next thing we get is a report to the effect that the Carthaginian fleet, under Hamilco, had actually discovered the paradise in question. A likely explanation of this is that Hamilco's ships had come across the Madeira Islands, and brought back such a glowing account of their climate and vegetation, that public opinion jumped to the conclusion that this was that Abode of the Just their forefathers had talked about. They promptly

christened them the Fortunate Isles. This conviction persisted for
hundreds of years. The medieval geographers began to put these
mysterious islands on their maps, and several attempts were made
to discover and colonize them. In fact, treaties were drawn up ar-
ranging for their annexation when found.

According to a chart of the fourteenth century, they were situated among the Canaries or the Dog Islands. But in Brendan's time,
they were supposed to lie due west of Ireland. He knew all about
them, we may be sure, because a Celtic folktale of great antiquity
speaks of these jewels set in the nearby seas. Those who frequent
the Kerry coast will tell you that, in certain conditions of the at-
mosphere, it is extremely difficult to distinguish between earth,
sea, and sky; that sea and sky often combine to look like real and
solid land. As for the local inhabitants, they maintain that there is
no doubt about it at all; that, from where they live, the Enchanted
Country can be seen, once every seven years, poised like a fairy-
city on the far horizon's verge.

Whatever way it was, then, and whatever his motive, the day
came when the watchers on shore saw the sails of Brendan's boat
growing smaller and smaller, until they disappeared at last beneath
the rim of the western ocean. There were eighteen stout men and
true on board, and in the cargo they had a keg of Irish butter with
which they intended to grease the vessel's sides . . .

∞

Seven years later, the New Odysseus and his followers arrived
back safe and sound in the Bay of Tralee. There was nothing unusual about that. Such prolonged absences were the order of the
day among these brethren of the cloister. When they discovered a
new territory, they generally made a serious attempt to convert the
native population. It was not flying visits they paid to the Orkneys

and Shetlands, to St. Kilda's, to the Faröe Islands and Iceland; that is proved by the traces they left behind, some of which have lasted down to our own day.

And that Brendan and his crew had a tale to tell on arrival, and an exciting tale, stands to reason. It would be dead against nature to expect sailors to hold their tongues after voyaging for so long on unexplored seas.

"Arrah! Come on, now! Tell us about this land of yours that you say is full of strange things and strange people. Where does it lie?"

"Where does it lie? It lies out there; straight out there where the sun is setting."

"Far out?"

"Yes, far enough. We sailed for four months before we came to the belt of mist."

"What mist?"

"God alone knows what mist. I can only say that for twenty days we were swallowed up in it, without being able to see the blades of our own oars."

"And then you came to this land of mystery, as you call it?"

"No, not at once. A lot happened before that. We passed through a land of perpetual day, where the setting sun only hides itself for a short time, so that there is no real night or darkness at all. It was in this place that we saw huge islands made of solid ice floating like boats in the water, and splitting up into pieces that drifted apart on their own. We saw other ice islands with mountains on them belching forth smoke and fire, and others again surrounded by water so transparent that you could look down almost to the sea-bed, where mighty monsters were swimming to and fro. One island we saw was carpeted with green grass growing down to the very verge of the waves, and another was guarded by sentinels in the shape of animals sixty to eighty feet long, spouting steam and water into the sky. We tied up at the next bit of land we came to. It was a friendly place, only it took us months to get used to the heat."

"Was it an island?"

"It might have been. Some of us climbed to the top of a high hill near where we landed, and there did seem to be water all around. But you can never be sure."

"What sort of a country was it?"

"Well, believe me, we saw sights there totally different from anything ever seen on this side."

"For instance?"

"Trees with trunks as thick as some of our churches; trees covered with marvelous flowers and fruit, and trees giving out a perfume that clung to our clothes for weeks after we left. And, do you know, the men and women are not white like us; they are brown, as brown as the hides covering the boat we sailed in. And it's little enough they have on them, I can tell you."

"But, surely, they were human beings like ourselves."

"That's the point — were they? They had the same bodies, to be sure, but I doubt if they had the same souls. They seemed to me to have no knowledge either of good or of evil. Happy-go-lucky, innocent grown-up children: that's the idea of them I carried away."

And so on and so on.

This is no more than the bare outline of the tale Brendan may be supposed to have told. Examined in detail, it is seen to contain no statement that is not a plain statement of fact. We happen to know that. Our own explorers have told us about that first impression of innocency and childishness made upon the European by negroes and redskins, and primitive races generally, the impression of a people never serious and always at play. Those, too, who are in the habit of crossing the North Atlantic are familiar enough with these prolonged sea-fogs, that are apt to hold up even modern shipping. But Brendan's contemporaries were not acquainted with such things, least of all with the arctic phenomena brought to light in his story: the midnight sun, the floating icebergs, the transparent water, and the spouting whales. They knew of no trees as thick as Brendan's trees, and of no men and women whose faces were as brown as the hides the boats of the day were covered with.

One item, in particular, made the monks prick up their ears.

"I think you said you sailed for some months through a belt of mist."

"We did that."

"Well, I'm surprised that you made no attempt to find out what that mist was covering. It's my belief that you were all but within reach of the Land of Everlasting Youth, the island to which the Spirit of Truth and the Spirit of Justice fled when they forsook our world."

"Maybe so. But if it was, the likes of us couldn't have landed; it is guarded by the souls of the just and the wings of the angels."

"No heathen could have landed, I grant you, because it is barred to those who carry the curse of the earth upon them. But we Christians have been redeemed from that curse. I tell you, I would have landed, risk or no risk. And didn't you say that there was no such thing as darkness in that locality?"

"Well, there was practically none to speak of."

"Exactly! And don't all the ancient books describe that blessed island as a place in which the sun never sets? Ah, Father Abbot, what a chance you missed there! What a chance!"

And so the tale was unfolded, bit by bit, Brendan describing what he and his companions had seen, in particular the customs and habits of the people whose hospitality they had enjoyed for so long. There the Abbot's responsibility ended. What interpretation his listeners might choose to put upon his matter-of-fact story was none of his affair. And what posterity might choose to do with his story was none of his affair.

Sure enough, around the extraordinary although veracious account of this voyage, the Celtic imagination soon grouped a whole cycle of myths. In the tenth century, they were committed to writing by an anonymous scribe, with a poetic gift that makes his book one of the outstanding creations of the human mind. This Latin production passed into the literature of Europe, and was translated into French, German, Danish, Italian, Norwegian, and English. A version of it must have reached Persia, for two stories from it are to be found in the *Arabian Nights* — namely, Sinbad's adventures on the Island of Sheep and on the Island of Birds. This ingenious Celtic writer, whoever he was, did for Brendan what Homer did for the heroes of ancient Greece. It is not unreasonable to suppose that Ulysses and Achilles were real personages, figuring in the primitive history of that land. It may be that the traditions and memories of their exploits provided the raw material of those great poems. The *Voyage of Brendan* is a kind of Odyssey, in a way, whose hero is a Christian saint.

It is this circumstance that accounts for the difference between the two compositions. Homer's story abounds in deeds of violence and revenge; in the other, there is hardly a single cruel idea; all is lovely, pure, and acceptable. So much so that one critic says of it, "Never has a gaze so benevolent and so gentle been cast upon the earth." Evil appears under the form of monsters wandering in the deep, or of Cyclopes confined in volcanic islands; but God causes them to destroy one another, and does not permit them to hurt the good. Pity and mercy are extended even to those who might be thought to have gone beyond the reach of pity and mercy. On a rock, in the midst of the Polar Seas, they find Judas; and it turns out that, on account of an act of charity he once performed, he is allowed to pass one day of the week in this place of refreshment, with the cloak he had given to the beggar hung up to protect him from the wind. When Brendan came to the Isle of Birds, he discovered that these creatures, who joined with his monks in singing the Office, were really the Fallen Angels or, rather, those of the Fallen Angels who had not quite rebelled. As an act of clemency, they had been changed into birds and banished to this island. On the Isle of Sheep, they found these animals governing themselves according to their own laws, without any interference from man. On the Isle of Delight an absolute stillness reigned, and no one on it could feel either cold or heat; time itself was in a state of suspended animation, because the sun remained forever stationary in its meridian tower.

Putting all this poetry on one side, the question still remains: What exactly was this country that Brendan visited during his long absence, a country evidently foreign enough in manners and appearance to give rise to the legends that came after? Could it have been some outpost of the New World — one of the Bahamas, for example — or even the mainland of America itself? Who knows? What we do know is that, on the strength of the story Brendan had to tell, the existence of an immense territory, watered by a great river and lying to the west of Ireland, now became an article of faith with medieval geographers.

Some Icelandic historians do ascribe the first discovery and Christianization of the North American coast to the Irish monks of Brendan's time; in fact, that same coast is named by them *Irland it Mikla,* or Greater Ireland. When the Spanish *Conquistadores* arrived in Mexico, at the beginning of the sixteenth century, they were astonished to find dim but unmistakable traces of the Christian religion. On inquiring into the origin of these beliefs and practices, they were told how, many centuries before, a mysterious white man had arrived in their country from the east, that he was dressed in a long tunic covered with crosses, and that he preached a new religion inculcating penance and self-denial. Having taught the Mexicans to venerate the Cross, "on which a Man more resplendent than the sun had died," he sailed away from the Gulf of Mexico, going in the direction of the rising sun or, as he told them, returning to the place he had come from. The natives called this stranger Quetzalcoatl; and they declared that, before leaving, he foretold that the Spaniards would come, someday, and take possession of their country.

Who was this Quetzalcoatl? Was he, by any chance, a Kerry man born near Tralee? Was he, by any chance, the monk known to posterity as Brendan the Navigator?

Several mysteries will be cleared up in the next world; this will be one of the minor ones.

∞

Druids' Last Stand

Columba, the greatest of all the saints of Scotland, was well past middle age when he put his hand to the most important enterprise of his career.

On the eve of Pentecost, in the year 563, he and twelve companions had landed on Iona, a small island of the Inner Hebrides, formerly the headquarters of the local Druids. This refuge, which was less than six square miles in extent, had been made over to him by a relative of his own, the Chief of the Dalriad Scots. These latter were Irishmen who had occupied that part of Scotland some time before.

Banishment from his native land had been imposed upon Columba, as a penance for the loss of life resulting from a dispute in which he had been involved; but it was required of him, besides, that in his place of exile he should devote his remaining years to the work of converting the heathen.

Columba's fellow-countrymen and fellow-Christians, the Scots of Argyllshire, still required a good deal of religious attention; but, at any rate, they were not unbelievers. However, not so very far away, lying north and east of the Grampian chain of mountains, there was a people still obstinately pagan. These were they who lived in what the Romans termed Caledonia, a place-name which makes its literary appearance, for the first time, in a Latin poem written in the year 60 by the poet Lucan. The word still survives, for instance, in Dunkeld, which is the Fortification of the Caledonians.

Caledonia was the abode of the Northern Picts, a branch of a great race of disputed origin, probably Scandinavian, formerly occupying many parts of Great Britain. Their name, it seems, has nothing to do with paint, but may be derived from the particular kind of boat in which they had carried on their trade of piracy. Together with the Scots, they divided between them the greater part of what is now known as Scotland: the Southern Picts living on the banks of the Forth and in the districts south of that river, and the Northern Picts remaining undisputed masters of the region lying beyond the Backbone of Britain, as the Grampians were called. Tacitus, the ancient historian, described the latter as the most remote of all the earth's inhabitants, and the last champions of freedom — a reference to the fact that they alone had successfully withstood the advance of the Roman legions.

Difficult to conquer, they were difficult to convert; and for one and the same reason: they just could not be got at. Their headquarters were at Inverness, where the probable site of their stronghold is still pointed out: Craig Phadrig, a rocky eminence over four hundred feet above sea-level, standing close to where the River Ness formerly flowed into the Moray Firth. Here King Brude held his court surrounded by the pick of his warriors.

How to reach this fortress was the question that remained to be solved. Fortunately, there was in the Iona community a monk who knew that part of Caledonia well and could speak the Pictish dialect fluently. This was Canice, or Kenneth, the same who was the first to preach the gospel in what is now St. Andrews. Kenneth was therefore sent for, and presently he and Columba were in conference together.

"Rise from your knees," said the Abbot, "seat yourself and listen. This night an angel has taught me that it is God's will that I go to Brude; for if the shepherd be once converted, the sheep will follow as a matter of course."

"But, Father, this Brude is a fierce and warlike prince, and he lives perched upon a pinnacle like an eagle on its nest."

"No matter. He must be won over, and the sooner, the better. Would you have me shrink back from one who is destined to lead a whole race of people to eternal life? I want you to advise me, Kenneth, not to dissuade me. You must be my guide as well, for you know those parts, and I do not. I command you in the name of God."

"Yes," was the reply. "I know those parts and know them only too well. Without the visible protection of Heaven, no stranger will ever succeed in reaching the Pictish stronghold. Caledonia that country was well named, for it is truly a Land of Forests; and they are such forests, I tell you, that an army might lose itself in them and be never heard of again."

"No doubt! But, you see, I do count on the visible protection of Heaven; and, besides, I propose to leave the forests alone. You told me once of the lochs. You said once that, with some contrivance, resolute men might go from sea to sea by way of the lochs; from our sea here in the west to the northern sea, where Brude has his fortress. We are resolute men, and we shall contrive to go by the lochs. Have you anything more to say?"

"Yes, I have this to say. Before you can come at Brude, you will have to cross a sheet of water more than twenty miles in length."

"What then?"

"The Druids have put a spell upon that water, a spell fatal to every stranger who ventures to sail it. The spell is so strong that

Brude has no need of soldiers to guard his fortress; he leaves it to the spell. So I have been told."

"Well, my son, we shall put a spell on their spell. So, have no fear. My Druid is Christ, the Son of God. *Air a' ghabh sinn biodh* — Let it be as arranged."

And so it was decided.

∞

The lochs in question have since been linked together to form the Caledonian Canal, which cuts Scotland in two. Thanks to this piece of excavation, there is now nothing to prevent a boat from sailing, say, out of Oban, and getting to Inverness without having to go around by the Shetland Islands. But, in Columba's day, these waterways were separated by stretches of wild territory, thickets of heather, and dense woods of pine, through which no vessel of any size could possibly be transported. Columba resolved to put a good coracle or skiff on board — one, that is to say, capable of floating three persons. When the time came for the three in question to take to the road, they would carry the coracle from one loch to another, leaving the long-boat, meanwhile, to pick them up on their return.

Fortunately, the monks of Iona were expert both at building ships and at sailing them. They needed to be, for they had chosen to take up their abode in a region where the sea, like an absolute monarch, penetrates and dominates everything. If missionary work was to be carried on at all, this absolute monarch had to be mastered in his turn. This was well understood by all, and understood from the first day of the landing. For the bulk of the community, Iona was never intended to be much more than the rallying point of a missionary come-and-go, a come-and-go that was to last for centuries. This spiritual traffic could be only by water; the nature and the situation of the rallying point saw to that. Boats, then, there had to be, and not ordinary boats either. Some hold that the name *Iona* means "Isle of the Waves," a testimony at once to the strength of the current flowing between it and its neighbor Mull, and also to the fury of the Atlantic breakers beating upon its western shore.

No sooner, then, was Columba's monastery built — a bunch of beehive cells constructed of clay, timber, and wicker-work thatched with reeds, and grouped around an oratory or church — than the monks erected a shipbuilding yard and began to make boats. In the end, they had a fleet of these; and of the 150 monastics the island soon contained, no fewer than seventy were to devote their attention to the business of navigation. Their boats were of two kinds: coracles made of osier and covered with skins, and heavy vessels, hollowed out of the trunks of trees, which went with sail or oar and were furnished with masts and rigging.

The Abbot himself made a careful study of tides and storms, and everything connected with weather forecasts; so much so that the fisher-folk of the west had recourse to him for advice and warnings. Iona, in fact, was a kind of meteorological office. Land or water, it was all the same to Columba; if anything, he and his were even more at home on the water than on the land. In a poem composed in the Gaelic tongue he reveals his partiality.

> *What joy to fly upon the white-crested sea,*
> *And to watch the waves break upon the shore!*
> *What joy to row the little bark,*
> *And land among the whitening foam!*

In fact, it has been said of Columba that, in art, his identity would best be determined by showing him standing near the sea, with a coracle in the foreground. And, sure enough, on an ancient

Christians Courageous

Scottish seal we see him seated in an open boat and gazing at the pilot stars.

Having made his calculations, the Abbot announced that the expedition would set out at dawn on June 2. This left those concerned with only a couple of weeks to make their preparations.

The first thing was to overhaul the vessel in which they intended to make the seagoing portion of the journey — from Iona, that is to say, around the Ross of Mull, through the Firth of Lorne, and so to the far end of Loch Linne. Linne means "pool," and, in fact, this so-called lake is really only one of the numerous deep incisions that the wind and sea between them have made in the western coast of Scotland. Getting to the top of this incision from Iona meant a voyage of about fifty miles, allowing for everything.

And quite a lot had to be allowed for. The sea-passage in question was one of the most dangerous in that welter of dangers. It was only one degree less perilous than the alternative route: northward from Iona, and around by Tobermory into the Sound of Mull. It was on that course that some of the stout ships of the Spanish Armada met with disaster. Southward from Iona and around the Ross, or Cape, of Mull meant risking the frightful currents sweeping downward through the Firth of Lorne, and threatening to drive them as far as the Cauldron of Brechan, or Corryvreckan, a whirlpool named after an Irish prince, a relative of Columba, who had perished there some years before.

The choice, therefore, was not a comforting one. This part of Scotland is so full of corridors, so to say, that it is one of the draftiest localities in the world, a place where the winds run riot and break all the rules. Gales come down through the deep glens of the mainland, and rival gales blow off the mountain ranges of the larger islands. Even on the calmest of calm days, the sea here is made treacherous, in spite of itself, owing to the presence of so many obstructions. It is useless looking for these obstructions in an atlas; no general atlas could possibly find room for those of them that are little more than clusters of bare rocks, or splintered pinnacles of basalt and granite, cleaving the air like the spires of our churches. Looking at an ordinary atlas, one could never believe that there are 365 islands off the Irish coasts. By that way of it, there must be three times that number off the west coast of Scotland. And these obstructions keep the waters hot and bothered all the while. If a small boat is to weather the shocks coming from so many directions, it has to be exceptionally sound and must be oarmanned as well as furnished with a sail.

There were other perils besides. In these remote seas, boats were liable to be attacked by certain shellfish, which attached themselves to the skin-covered sides and made dangerous perforations. At that period, too, whales swarmed about the Hebrides, and sharks ascended the rivers and fjords of the west coast — formidable monsters, nearly thirty feet long, similar to the basking sharks that still infest the seas off the west coast of Ireland, and whose oil the natives use for their lamps. These have been known to chase fishing-boats for miles, and, in one case, a man had to abandon his coracle and hide in a cave for some hours until the shark got tired of waiting.

But the monks of Iona knew what they were about. The vessel chosen for the sea trip was one of those strongly built craft that the first biographer of Columba, Adamnan by name, calls a *navis oneraria*. It had been hollowed out of an oak tree of immense girth ferried across from Skye. This island was much favored by Columba and, at that date, was practically uninhabited. One of its smaller lakes is called after him, and for hundreds of years, he was invoked as the patron saint of the islanders.

Christians Courageous

The coracle, on which they were to depend for the second part of the journey, was made of wicker, lined within and without with hide. It was what was known as a three-skin coracle, which meant that it was big enough to hold three. Propelled by a couple of light paddles made of ash, it was portable and added very little weight to the main cargo. It was provided with plank seats; and, when you wished to transport it from one place to another, you tipped it up on end, slipped head and shoulders under one of the planks, and walked off looking rather like a soldier carrying his own sentry-box.

When the day drew near, a crew of eight of the most experienced mariners was chosen, with the monk Cormac in charge. He had sailed as far as the Faröe Isles and the Orkneys, and had a cool head and a practiced eye. With Columba as super-cargo went Comgall, a veteran missionary; and, of course, the aforesaid Canice, or Kenneth, who was to act as guide and interpreter in one.

Before embarking, Columba addressed them from the water's edge. "Let us," he said, "exert ourselves as though everything depended on us, and let us pray as though everything depended on the Almighty." Then followed the Invocations, a kind of litany, addressed to all the known saints, beginning with Jonah, who in various times and places had gone down to the sea in ships.

And with that they set sail.

Those who have never viewed these western islands from an open boat at sunrise on a summer's day can form no idea of the panorama that opened up as soon as the island of Iona was cleared. On land and water, neither cloud nor mist was to be seen. As they pulled around the bend, they had a fleeting glimpse of Staffa, where Fingall's cave is; of Treshinish and Ulva, and the long stretches of Tiree and Coll. With Iona left behind, there loomed up to the south Oronsay, where Columba had first landed on coming from Ireland, Colonsay nearby, and farther off, Islay and the Paps of Jura. Islands everywhere. And surrounding them, the unflagging energy of the sea.

They were now entering upon an ordeal that was to test alike their skill and their powers of endurance. The sail was unfurled and the oars were planted in the thole-pins; massive ash-sweeps these oars were, which only strong men were capable of handling. Columba prayed aloud and then, to cheer his companions, he recited a portion of his "Song of Trust," a poem that, for centuries, was to be the standby of travelers, by land as well as water:

> A guard may guide him on his way;
> But can they, can they guard
> Against the touch of death?
> Better is He in whom we trust;
> The King who made us all.
> For God's elect are safe,
> Even in the front of battle.

For hours on end, they pulled and pulled in a contest with the currents, where a momentary failure might have brought disaster. At last, the worst was over and, when Cormac had hoisted the sail, the oarsmen lay across the thwarts like dead men. It was as well that they did so, because one other big effort had to be made.

The day was well advanced when they passed out of the Firth of Lorne, so named after Loarn, the first king of the Dalriad Scots, and drew near to Lismore. In the thirteenth century, this island was the seat of a bishopric; but the stormy channel separating it from the mainland led to the transfer of the episcopal dwelling; the third occupant of the see was drowned here in 1241. Once again, therefore, the sail was let down, and the tired monks had to negotiate a small but very awkward corner. They did it by keeping close in to the Lyon, or Domain, of Lorne, until they had pulled beyond the northern extremity of the island. Then, turning backward on the tide, they allowed it to carry them to their destination. On Lismore they spent the night, the conical peak of Ben Cruachan standing sentinel some distance away.

The next stage was plain sailing, the distance from Lismore to the end of Loch Linne being about thirty miles. But this time, wind and tide were in their favor, so that, before long, they had passed the dense forest of Mamore, and come to rest on a shelving reach of sand close to Inverlochy, where the Marquis of Montrose defeated the Covenanters in 1645.

Here the ship's company were to divide and separate. The crew returned to Lismore in the transport, with instructions to wait for ten days, and then set out for the rendezvous, near Inverlochy, in order to pick up the three missionaries. The latter — Columba, Canice, and Comgall — shouldered their coracle and pushed on across the six or seven miles of forest land intervening between Loch Linne and Loch Lochy, or the Dark Loch. This was navigated without mishap. There was another overland trek before they reached Loch Oich, and at its head they spent the night, preparing for the biggest undertaking the coracle had to encounter.

At daybreak, they were afloat once more with a formidable run of nearly thirty miles before them. The mountain torrents, coming down from the high ground where the snow had just melted, were in full spate, and the air was filled with the noise they made as they tumbled at last into the loch. Some of them were swollen to the size of considerable rivers which, pouring into this great reservoir of waters, produced an agitation that set the coracle bouncing and bobbing like a cork. And corks indeed they were, these rough-and-ready craft into whose simple construction years of experience had been put. They responded to the merest flick of the paddles, and would turn or stop, accelerate or slow down at will.

As Kenneth had warned Columba, the loch they were now on was sacred to the Druids, whose priests were credited with being able to put spells and enchantments even on inanimate nature. And, sure enough, it was not easy to account for the accumulation of obstacles that now began to beset the path of the three missionaries. Again and again, they were molested by a strange marine monster, serpent-shaped, which followed them like a beast of prey. There were other hindrances, besides, and in particular, a gale of wind and a dense fog that met them at the narrow extremity, where the loch makes way for the river. But Columba exhorted his followers to be brave, and to encourage them, he recited again snatches of his "Song of Trust":

> O Royal Sun, prosper my path,
> And then I shall have nothing to fear.
> My life?
> As God pleases let it be;
> Nought can be taken from it,
> Nought can be added to it:
> The lot which God has given,
> Ere a man dies must be lived out.
> He who seeks more, were he a prince,
> Shall not a mite obtain.
> My Druid is Christ, the Son of God,
> The Son of Mary; the great Abbot;
> The Father, the Son, and the Holy Spirit.
> Better is He in whom we trust,
> The King who has made us all.

Christians Courageous

Just as Columbus quieted the Atlantic breakers by reading to them the first chapter of St. John's Gospel, so did the Abbot of Iona bid wind and wave, mist and monster, render obedience to the will of Him who holds them in the hollow of His hand:

> O Royal Sun, prosper any path,
> And then I shall have nothing to fear.

Columba had carried with him from Iona one of those little square bells, made of beaten iron, which the Celtic monks of those far-off days used in their monasteries. This he now rang, again and again, as though to challenge the evil spirits. "For these bells of ours," he reminded his followers, "are the trumpets of the Church Militant, and the time to sound them is when we are approaching the enemy's stronghold."

This they were certainly doing, and at considerable speed too. The coracle had parted from the loch, and had entered the swiftly flowing waters of the river Ness which, before long, provided them with a distant view of their objective. There it was, away to the left, a plateau showing above the tallest trees, and surmounted by a fortress whose frowning walls were lighted up by the rays of the evening sun. Within an hour they were alongside. Springing ashore, they drew the coracle up to a place of safety, and then made their way through the undergrowth to the rough track leading to the summit, whose base was, at that time, about a mile from the head of the river. Sign or sound of a human being there was none. But when they had climbed to the top and were approaching the entrance to the castle, they could see the men-at-arms moving about upon its walls. On being challenged by these, Kenneth advanced to within earshot and, speaking in the Pictish tongue, demanded an audience of the king. "We are men of peace," he said, "and it is a message of peace that we bring with us." The request was refused.

Columba now took things into his own hands. Drawing himself up to his full height, he began to intone the forty-fourth psalm. It was the first time the words of Scripture had found utterance in that part of Scotland. And it was the first time the Northern Picts became acquainted with that famous voice whose conversational tones, we are told, could be heard at a distance of a thousand paces. As its deep intonations rolled across the valley, and echoed from hill to hill, the superstitious warriors looked up at the sky to see where the thunder was coming from. In vain did Broichan, the king's chief magician, order the drums and cymbals to be beaten; the voice rose and rose, like a tide, sweeping before it all opposition. Its effect upon the great oak postern was like that of a battering-ram. The timbers shook and shuddered, and ended by bursting open. The three monks entered the presence-chamber like conquerors coming to dictate terms.

This wonder made so deep an impression on the monarch that he consented to listen to the words the Abbot addressed to him through Kenneth, the interpreter. It is not recorded that he became a Christian; but, during the rest of his life, he remained the friend and protector of Columba, and allowed him to move freely through his dominions.

In this way it was that a missionary movement was begun that extended to the whole of Caledonia, leaving memorials of Columba's presence in nearly every part of that area. In this way it was that the prophecy he uttered shortly before his death was well advanced toward fulfillment at the very time he was making it. Already Pict and Scot, once so sharply divided, were united in their veneration for Iona, that spot "so small and so low," which had given the faith to the one and had consolidated the faith of the other.

∞

Caedmon

It would be impossible to overrate the services rendered to Christian England by St. Augustine and his fellow Benedictines who, landing near Ramsgate in the year 597, inaugurated their apostolate by converting Ethelbert, together with thousands of his subjects. At the same time, to ignore the contribution made to the common cause by the Celtic monks would present a very one-sided view of the picture. Of the eight kingdoms that made up the Anglo-Saxon confederacy, Kent was the only one that owed nothing to their ministrations. They were active in Wessex, East Anglia, and even in Sussex; while their influence was paramount in Essex, Mercia, and Northumbria, which, between them, accounted for more than two-thirds of the whole country.

It is true that Paulinus, one of Augustine's assistants, successfully preached the gospel in the northern kingdom and baptized its ruler Edwin. But when the same ruler lost his life, in the disastrous battle of Heathfield, the bishop had to fly south and exchange the See of York for that of Rochester. It was King Oswald who retrieved the political situation by defeating Cadwalla. With a view to retrieving the religious situation, the Irish monk Aidan traveled all the way from the Hebrides and fixed his headquarters at

Lindisfarne. This island, which in size and appearance closely resembles Iona, became the spiritual capital of the north and the residence of its first sixteen bishops.

In spite of a number of ups and downs, the venture steadily
prospered. The Christian Faith struck deep roots in this rugged
soil, and mission-stations began to spring up all over the territory
lying between the Humber and the Tweed. In this work of exten-
sion, King Oswy was particularly active. When, eventually, Pen-
da's defeat had decided the fate of England, he signalized his
victory by making a grant of land, for the upkeep of a religious
house to be erected in one of the most picturesque localities of the
Yorkshire coast. This was in 657.

At the spot where the river Esk enters the North Sea, there is a
circular bay surmounted by lofty cliffs. On the summit of one of
these, there soon arose an imposing group of wooden buildings,
conforming in appearance to the Celtic idea of a monastery. The
main structure, consisting of a church, a refectory, and the lodgings of the actual community, was surrounded by a rampart and a
ditch. Outside this enclosure were the various agricultural de-
pendencies: the cattle-sheds, the barn, the kiln for drying the
grain, the mill with its pond and stream, the smithy, the carpen-
ter's shop, and, of course, a regular village of wattle huts, occupied
by the servants and retainers who contributed to form the religious clan or family. Whitby the place came to be called later, but
its original name was Streonshalh, or "Isle of the Beacon," the
conjecture being that the first superior of this monastery had
placed a lighthouse on the edge of the cliff.

This first superior was no other than Hild, or Hilda, a princess
of royal blood, a relation of King Edwin and one of the greatest
Englishwomen of all time. She took charge of the new foundation,
which was something the pioneers of Irish monasticism had not

dreamed of — namely, a double-monastery. At Whitby, men and women, although occupying separate quarters, were striving to serve God as one community, and were living under the authority, not of a monk, but of a nun — an arrangement that seems to have made its first appearance in Gaul.

Thanks to the inspiration and wise government of Hilda, this wild corner of our northern seaboard became famous as a religious center, and was a training ground for bishops and missionaries. At one time, it was nicknamed Presby, on account of the number of priests congregated there, just as, among surviving place-names, we have Prescot, Preston, Presteigne, and Prestwick, all derived apparently from the same circumstance. St. John of Beverley and St. Wilfred of York were educated under the watchful eye of the Abbess. Kings and princes often came to her for advice; while, on the other hand, so much consideration was shown even to the humblest of her farm laborers, that Whitby was pointed out as a model of what a Christian community ought to be.

Among these latter was a certain cowherd who, without in the least suspecting it, was destined to achieve immortality, and literary immortality at that. For years, he had toiled away at the menial tasks allotted to him, differing from his associates in nothing save the use he made of his leisure. The long summer evenings he usually spent at the foot of the lighthouse, watching the ebb and flow of the tide, with a glimpse caught, now and then, of the brown sails of a fishing-boat. In bad weather, he would shelter in a nearby oak-grove, and listen to the song the Esk kept singing, as it rushed over the rocks and pebbles, before fanning out to make its entry into the sea. Farther upstream, a certain pool was a great favorite of his. He would lie flat on the bank and gaze for hours on end into its glassy depths; and, noticing how, on bright days, it mirrored the blue sky overhead, he would think how in this it resembled the human soul reflecting the image of its Creator. At nighttime, too, he often rose from his pallet, while his companions slept, in order to contemplate the shining wonders of the firmament. But perhaps his happiest hours were passed out there in what was left of the primeval forest. So dense was it that its paths were known only to the few; but he was one of the few, and he came and went among its wild inhabitants without fear on either side. Squirrels had their homes in the tree-trunks, adders in the rich earth beneath them, and, in the great heats, the glades were alive with humming.

Nature and he were on the best of terms, except for one thing. The setting sun, the starlit sky, the sparkling waters — all these seemed to beckon to him, as though they wished to borrow his voice, to make him their mouthpiece, their spokesman. And he had no voice; he had only a mouth that was dumb. He to whom they gave so much could give nothing in return. At harvest-time, the sharp ring of the reapers' scythes made a music in his heart; but this music, for want of an instrument, would straightway die down and be lost.

It was the same with the great sights he had seen taking place in the abbey. He had witnessed the burial service of Edwin, as well as that of Oswy, his successor; the bodies of the two monarchs reposed, side by side, in the church. Before that, he had been a spectator of the greatest ecclesiastical turnout Anglo-Saxon England had so far experienced. In 664, the Council of Whitby, over which the king himself presided, brought together all the Christian elements in the nation and resounded with the eloquence of its spiritual leaders who were, at the time, at variance on certain matters of church discipline. Events such as these stirred him even more than the pageant of nature; but when he attempted to express these emotions of his soul, the syllables seemed to take fright and flee away into silence.

In the latter part of July, everybody rose early and worked as long as there was light to see with. But as soon as the Hlaf-Maess, or Loaf Mass, had been celebrated, it was the will of the Abbess that during Lammas-tide the tired laborers should enjoy a period of relaxation. The liberty of each day was crowned by an entertainment during which the harp — always an important item in the inventory of a Celtic monastery — was passed from hand to hand, and the company diverted themselves listening to the old ballads handed down by their forefathers. They were mostly about battles and feuds and forays; rhyming fragments that had taken shape before Britain was invaded; stories of the continental days featuring, not the Humber and the Tyne, but the Eider and the Elbe. There were sea songs as well, and snatches of rustic poetry, and versified riddles, describing some bird or beast or natural phenomenon, which tested the guessing powers of the listeners, and were the most popular of all. Some of these themes were not at all to the taste of the cowherd; but, in any case, with this chronic impediment of his, he could do no other than stand aloof from the minstrelsy.

One night, being pressed to take the harp and sing something of his very own, and finding that he could not, he slipped out of the great hall; and, since the farm horses were in his charge that week, he retired to the stable and composed himself to rest among the beasts. His last waking thoughts were tinged with the old regrets: he yearned to be able to call speech and song to his aid, as did his companions — with this difference, however: he would use his endowment to celebrate the doings, not of Hengist and Horsa, but of the Prince of Peace and the sainted heroes of His Church. Somewhere at the back of his mind there lingered the memory of one whose lips an angel had purified with a burning coal, and of another who complained to God: "Ah, ah, ah! I cannot speak, for

I am but a child." And, with closed eyes and joined hands, he prayed, as often he had heard the monks praying:

> Domine, labia inea aperies,
> Et os meum annuntiabit laudem tuam.
>
> Thou shalt open my lips, O Lord,
> And my mouth shall declare Thy praise.

When he awakened at dawn, it was to find that he had been cradled into poetry while he slept. This frustrated man, who, when the harp went around, could only stammer out excuses, was now weaving verses as though to the manner born; weaving them, too, into a pattern of his very own. The jingle of the rhyme was the old jingle heard in the land these many years; but the heathen themes had been exchanged for new ones, for Christian ones. God, apparently, had stepped down from His high Heaven and was seating Himself on the throne hitherto occupied by Wotan or Thor. And, just as of old this God was fond of taking His prophets from the sheepfold, so now, for His formal entry into English poetry, He had chosen for escort a farmhand who could neither read nor write.

Before long, the wonder came to the ears of the grieve, or bailiff; and he, as in duty bound, reported it to his mistress, the Abbess Hilda, who appointed an hour at which inquiry was to be made into the mystery. And since she was fully persuaded that poetry is in some sort a sacred thing, she had summoned to her side those of her community who were men of spiritual discernment, besides being skilled in the musical art. When the cowherd stood before them, she bade him tell his tale in his own way.

"Fear and favor," she said, "have no admittance among us, and you may disregard the one as much as the other. How did this power come to you?"

"In the night; in a dream, or a vision, I hardly know which. Some person, whom I could not recognize, stood by my side and told me to sing, to sing some song."

"And what then?"

"I made answer that I had no gift of that kind in me. For all that, he insisted and would take no denial. 'Sing,' he said, 'and let your song be about the beginning of created things.' "

"And then you found yourself singing?"

"Yes, all at once, and in spite of myself almost. My lips just moved, and the sounds came."

"What sounds?"

"The sounds of good words falling into their right places, and making music as they fell; the words of our own tongue, telling the praises of Him who made the heavens and the earth."

"For instance?"

Nu scylum hergan hefaenricaes uard,
Metudes maecti end his modgidane,
Uerc uuldurfadur; sue he uundra gihuaes
Eci Dryctin or astelidae.

Now must we greet with praise the guard of Heaven's realm,
The Maker's might and of His mind the thought,
The glorious Father's Works, and how to wonders all
He gave beginning, He the Eternal Lord.

"And that was all?"

"Yes, that was all, at the time. But when morning came, I remembered everything and found, besides, that I could add verses of my own. I need pictures. If I have pictures, I can make the pictures speak."

The Abbess smiled at this and remained thoughtful.

"You shall have pictures in plenty," she said presently. And then she bade one of her monks who was learned in the Scriptures describe, in brief, some of the stirring events to be found in the sacred pages. And when he had done so, she turned to the cowherd: "We shall meet again in this place tomorrow at the same hour and, God willing, you will let us hear what these new pictures have to say for themselves."

When the appointed time came, an end was put to any doubts that remained. Formerly the infant Mercury, playing on the seashore, picked up a tortoise-shell and fashioned it into the first lyre. That was fable. What was sober fact was that some powerful, although unseen, hand had now passed over the rough substance of this peasant's soul, thereby fitting him to take his place at the head of the long muster-roll of our English poets. So manifest was the miracle that the Abbess persuaded the cowherd to embrace the monastic way of living, and thus consecrate his God-given talent to the service of religion. Once inside the cloister, the man who was ignorant before was soon taught the whole cycle of sacred history, beginning with the Creation and ending with the great truths of the Christian Faith. And he, "keeping in mind all he heard, and, as it were, chewing the cud, converted the same into most harmonious verse, and turned into pupils those who before had been his masters."

He was called Caedmon. His name appears in the calendar of the Anglo-Saxon saints, and it figures prominently in every history of our English literature. Northumbria eventually became the cultural center of Christian England; in the movement that made it so, Caedmon played no inconspicuous part.

∞

First into China

"But surely you would not wish me to write that down?"

"Why not?"

"Well, I understood you to say that this was to be a book not of legends but of history."

"So it is; and what I am telling you now is history. I saw it with my own two eyes."

"You saw a tortoise as big as one of the cupolas of our church? You realize that that means a diameter of about forty feet."

"I do."

"Very good! I shall write that down as well. I am concerned only for your good name. You told me that, out there in China, the physicians can tell the state of a patient's health simply by feeling the pulse. At the medical school here in our city, I was told yesterday that such a thing was impossible."

"My dear Brother, *impossible* is the word we use to describe anything at all that, so far, has not fallen within the range of our own petty experience. It is a dangerous word. Wrong things continue to be wrong because, forsooth, the righting of them is held to be *impossible*."

It was a beautiful May morning in the year 1330, and the speakers were two Franciscan friars, one of whom was seated before a writing-desk in the scriptorium of the convent at Padua. The church referred to was begun a century before, built to shelter the remains of St. Anthony. He was a Franciscan, the personal friend of St. Francis of Assisi himself; and the man who was so insistent as to the truth of his story about the tortoise was a certain Father Odoric, a member of the same Mendicant Order. He had just returned to Italy, after an absence of twelve years, during which time he had visited India, Burma, Sumatra, Java, Borneo, Cochin-China, and China proper. In this last-mentioned country, he had sojourned for three years. He had arrived back shortly before, and having a presentiment that his end was near, he had persuaded the archivist of the convent, Brother William of Solagna, to commit his experiences to writing. Such a commission was not to be set aside, since at that period, Europe was interested in nothing so much as the Far East; China and the Chinese were the topic of the hour.

This outbreak of curiosity originated in the doings of a famous Mongol warrior who entered upon his career of conquests in the early years of this same century, the thirteenth. Everything fell before him so that, before long, he assumed the title of emperor. Being noted for his consistency of purpose, he came to be known as Tchinghiz Kakhan, *tchinghiz* meaning "inflexible," and *kakhan* "supreme prince," as distinguished from a mere khan, who was a ruler, or official, of lesser importance. The Chinese naturally looked upon themselves as safe, thanks to the Great Wall, which had taken ten years to build and was nearly fifteen hundred miles in length. Tchinghiz, or Jenghiz, however, forced one of the passes bisecting the wall, and brought that vast dominion to its knees. In due course, he had subdued practically the whole of Asia, and had founded the Mongolian kingdom based on Karakoram. Under his immediate successors, the tide of invasion poured across the Urals, the Volga, and the Danube; so that, with the exception of a set-back at Wahlstadt, in Silesia, the Mongols could claim to have fought sixty-five victorious battles, between Korea and the Adriatic Gulf, and to have subdued no fewer than thirty-two nations.

The ease with which this son of a petty chieftain gained victories in such widely scattered areas was attributed to the mobility of his armed forces, as well as to his unrestrained ruthlessness. With him, massacre was a set policy, a policy he pursued even when dead. It was considered politically expedient to keep his decease a secret for some time, with the result that, when his remains were being carried across the country to their place of interment, every man, woman, and child who happened to be a spectator of the cortege was put to death. Moreover, those who succeeded Jenghiz were just as ruthless as he had been. It might be a far cry to Karakoram, but the name Jenghiz was on the lips of every European. And it was pronounced with bated breath.

When the heads of the Church sat in council at Lyons, in 1245, a resolution was passed to the effect that the Papacy should dispatch an embassy to the Mongol court, in an effort to arrest the tide of destruction threatening Christendom. It was even hoped that expeditions of this kind might lead to the conversion of these organized and intrepid barbarians. The choice of the Pope fell upon a Franciscan friar called John of Carpini, who, in spite of his age and infirmity, was destined to be the first European to reach the Far East in modern times. He was destined, too, to inaugurate a series of such expeditions that was to last for hundreds of years.

Friar John was sixty-five years of age, and so corpulent that any traveling he did had to be done on the back of a donkey. Nevertheless, he and his companion took to the road immediately. Leaving Lyons on Easter Day, they went by way of Basle to Stuttgart and Leipsic, and having crossed the Oder and the Vistula, and traversed Poland and Lithuania, they reached Moscow. Here they were informed that an advance guard of the Mongols was encamped on the bank of the Volga below Kazan. Pushing on, they made the passage of that river without mishap. The commander-in-chief not only entertained the two friars, but he provided them with a safe conduct and an escort. So far, they had covered over two thousand miles, and done it with surprising rapidity, considering the nature of the transport. As many miles again remained before them on a route winding over the Urals, through central Asia, across the Kirghiz Steppe, and so into the northern portion of the Chinese empire, otherwise Mongolia proper, where, not far from Lake Baikal, stood Karakoram, the stronghold of the Great Khan. They arrived here on July 22, 1246, only to learn that the successor of Jenghiz had just died, and that the new emperor would not ascend the throne until another month was over.

Friar John was a spectator of the coronation of Kuyuk, which was attended by four thousand ambassadors, and took place in a huge marquee made of cloth of gold supported by poles of the same metal. The city itself was a typical Tartar one, a city of tents. There might be as many as fifty thousand of these, and they were pitched to form regular streets and squares, replete with shops and baths, as well as dwelling-houses.

Then the day came when the Franciscan secured an audience, and proceeded to lay the Pope's message before the Great Khan. This was to the effect that the Tartars should leave off plundering and killing the Christians of the West, and should embrace the religion of the gospel. Kuyuk's reply is still preserved in a document that Carpini drew up at the time, written in Arabic and Latin. Its tone is haughty enough, but there is nothing threatening about it. "If you want peace," the Pope is told, "then come out here, and sue for it in person."

If this first contact between the European and the remote Asiatic failed in its immediate object, on a long-term view, it was one of the most successful undertakings of its kind ever taken in hand. Carpini bridged the gulf separating East and West. The name Cathay, which he used to designate the vast empire he had just visited, was now heard in our continent for the first time.

For some reason or another, the ancient Greeks and Romans remained profoundly ignorant of the world lying beyond the Urals and the Oxus, and of the Chinese in particular. They were familiar enough with one of their products — namely, silk; and to this commodity they gave the name of the people who manufactured it (Seres), just as we have given the name muslin to the fabric first woven in Mosul. But the European traders of old time probably bought their silks in the market of Samarkand, the capital of Sogdiana, which Alexander the Great invaded. This city, which contains the splendid tomb of Tamerlane, lay on the main route traversed by the silk caravans, and was a kind of halfway house between East and West. China is said to have sent an embassy to the Roman court in the time of Augustus, but there is no evidence that the compliment was ever returned. China was, and long remained, an unknown quantity.

Carpini put an end to all that. Over and above, the reports of what he had seen and heard stimulated the curiosity of our people and produced a succession of similar enterprises, some religious, some commercial. In this way the cause of knowledge was advanced, geographical and ethnological knowledge in particular. To give but one instance, a friar called Rubruck, who went out at this time from the court of King Louis of France, was the first to discover that the Caspian was an inland sea with no outlet to the Arctic at all.

Christians Courageous

In the end, everyone on this side was forced to admit that these remote peoples, hitherto thought to be savage and illiterate, were enjoying a very high degree of civilization, and had been doing so for hundreds of years. Marco Polo was one of those who helped in this way to put China on the map. His father and uncle had gone to Bokhara on business, and there they fell in with some envoys from the court of Kublai Khan. They were persuaded to accompany the envoys to China, and they were received by Kublai either at Cambaluc (Pekin) or at Shangtu. This Shangtu, ten days' journey from Pekin, was the summer quarters of the emperor, the Zanadu of Coleridge's poem:

> *In Zanadu did Kublai Khan*
> *A stately pleasure palace build.*

This was around about the year 1262. When the two brothers set out on their return, they carried letters in which Kublai requested the Pope to send one hundred educated men to instruct his subjects in the liberal arts and in the Christian Faith. Having delivered the letters, the brothers returned to China, along with Marco, then seventeen years old. This journey appears to have taken more than three years. On arrival, the three Italians were promptly enrolled in the public service; Marco, in particular, being employed on various delegations. When he appeared in Venice, some twenty years later, he was a rich man, rich in material wealth and rich in experience. He had visited Korea, Burma, Japan, and India, had crossed the Gobi Desert, and had made the acquaintance of lions, porcupines, cannibals, and pearl-divers.

Meanwhile the Pope had not forgotten Kublai's request, and in 1289, while Marco Polo was still residing in the Chinese capital, another Italian Franciscan was dispatched to the court of the emperor. This was John of Montecorvino, who went overland, as far as the Persian Gulf, and so by sea to India, where he tarried for over a year. He then embarked at Meliapore for Canton. He arrived in Pekin only to learn that Kublai was dead. His successor, however, made the friar welcome, and assigned him quarters near the royal palace, which occupied an area of four square miles. Everything prospered with this missionary, thanks to the personal friendship that developed between him and his royal host. He built two churches, as well as a college; and having purchased 150 Chinese boys, he taught them Latin and Greek, and formed them into a choir school. While these developments were in progress, he busied himself translating the New Testament and the Psalms into Chinese. In the end, John was made an archbishop.

It was at this stage of the intercourse between West and East that Odoric, the man who saw the forty-foot tortoise, made his appearance in Pekin. He ranks as one of the greatest travelers of all time. Embarking at Venice in a galley, in the spring of 1318, he sailed down the Adriatic, around Cape Matapan, and through the Aegean to Constantinople. From Constantinople, he went by sea to Trebisond, then through northern Asia Minor into Persia, where he received hospitality from his own brethren, who had a number of flourishing convents in that country. At the port of Hormuz, situated at the entrance to the Persian Gulf, he found a vessel about to set sail for India. After this, Odoric seems to have taken everything in his stride. He must have had a way with him, because, as soon as he got a notion that he would like to see this place or that, he apparently found those only too eager to provide him with ways and means of getting there. Sumatra, Java, Borneo, Burma, Cochin-China — few in fourteenth-century Europe knew of the existence of these territories, but Odoric made his way into each in turn, thanks to his Franciscan dress and his disarming personality.

His main objective, meanwhile, was China. Report had it that his confrère, John of Montecorvino, was actually ruling in the capital of this place, mitre and all. This was one of those incredible things worth traveling six or seven thousand miles to verify.

There were other incredible things waiting for him over there; and now, back in Padua at last, he was dictating some of the incredibilities to the scribe, Brother William of Solagna.

"You sailed, then, all the way from India to China?"

"Precisely! From Calicut to Canton. And in a vessel the like of which you never saw in your life. It was a three-sided affair, a triangle, and had four decks and seventy-two sails. It carried a crew of six hundred, besides four hundred soldiers. And, while you are at it, you may as well write down that it took thirty men to handle each oar, which was as big as a ship's mast. The rowers faced each other in two rows, and pulled on a chain fastened to the oar. As they rowed, they kept up a kind of chorus: 'La! La! La! La!' A fair amount of the food required was grown on board during the voyage, including pot herbs and ginger. The commander of the vessel was a great personage, a kind of emir or mandarin, and when he landed, the soldiers escorted him, led by their band. The Sea of China is so stormy that few ships ever get through. Hence, the sailors provide themselves with lifebelts, in the shape of bulls' hides, into which they are stitched. When the ships founder, these huge bladders float with the man inside and have a good chance of being washed ashore.

"They wanted me to believe," Odoric continued, "that they were carried ashore in the beaks of eagles. But you know what sailors are. I asked if anybody on board had ever actually witnessed the operation, or experienced it, and the answer was in the negative."

"How long did the voyage take?"

"Forty days."

"What happened when you landed?"

"I was received with the utmost civility, and told that I was welcome to the hospitality of the place, as long as I cared to stay, provided I respected the laws and customs of the country. I was lodged in an inn not far from the harbor. An official of some sort, clad from head to foot in the finest silk, accompanied me. Having carefully examined my belongings, he sealed up the inn for the night. Early next morning, he appeared at the door, broke the seals, checked my luggage, and asked if I had any complaint to make against the innkeeper. This procedure is followed wherever you are, with the result that in no country on earth is a stranger safer or more at his ease. To impose upon a traveler, in even the smallest way, they regard as criminal. You can travel anywhere without fear of being robbed."

"That's certainly more than you can do in Italy. But, proceed."

"I must tell you of another precaution they take, this time to protect themselves. The very first day I walked abroad, I noticed I was being shadowed by a number of men. They would study me closely and then, as I thought, write something in a scroll they carried. On inquiry, I learned that these were painters. The art of painting is carried to perfection in China, and nearly everybody paints. But these men were employed to paint by the state. As soon as a stranger arrives in the land, he is painted, often unknown to himself. These portraits are then displayed in the shop windows and posted up on the walls. They are such perfect likenesses that the original can be recognized at a glance. Should one of these strangers break the law, and then make his escape from the city, expert runners carry copies of his portrait right and left into the adjacent country, and especially to all frontier towns."

"You say that the officials are dressed in silk. How are the common people dressed?"

"In the same material. Silk seems to be the ordinary cloth out there. They think nothing of it. Jasper is a common stone with them. Tell a Chinaman that the walls of the New Jerusalem are made of jasper, and he won't be very much impressed."

"How are the grandees distinguished?"

"In many places by the length of their fingernails, and the women by the smallness of their feet. I saw a mandarin with his fingernails so overgrown that they completely encircled his hand. Some protect them by means of sheaths made of brass or silver. In certain districts, little girls belonging to the better class have their feet barbarously ill-treated, while they are young, so that they never grow any bigger. But the splendor amid which the great people live is almost unbelievable. The summer palace of the Great Khan, at Zanadu, is built of marble and precious stones, and surrounded by a park filled with deer. These they hunt, not with dogs, but with trained lynxes and leopards. I myself witnessed the funeral of an ordinary chief, and saw his immense tomb stored, not only with food and drink, but with the bodies of his horses and slaves slaughtered for the very purpose. However, here is something about China that will interest you, who are a scribe. In that country, they make books with far less labor than we devote to the making of them."

"In what way?" Brother William asked eagerly.

"Well, we can copy or write out only one book at a time. With the same initial labor, they can produce as many as they please."

"I still do not understand."

"Nor could I at first. But their secret is that they do not write the book by hand at all. They prepare large numbers of little blocks, like dice, made of wet clay, and on each block they fashion one letter; fashion it, too, in the most artistic manner. When the clay blocks have been baked in the oven, they arrange the blocks to form the words they require for the book, one sheet at a time. Each sheetful of words is fitted into a wooden frame and, when everything is arranged, the letters are inked over and stamped on paper. This printing, as it is called, has been in use among them for a very long period. I was shown a book, in the form of a roll sixteen feet long and one foot wide, which had been printed over four hundred years ago. It is highly esteemed as being the first production of its kind. In the beginning, the words required were carved on large wooden blocks, page by page. But they realized that waste could be avoided by making each letter a separate thing, and so combining the letters at will. This movable type is now everywhere in use."

This last item of information set Brother William thinking deeply. After a long silence, he expressed surprise that no European had, so far, thought of an invention that seemed simple enough, as long as you knew how it was done.

"It will come, never fear," Odoric assured him. "Before long, we shall see machines turning out books by the hundred. These Chinese have many things to teach us. They were familiar with gunpowder hundreds of years before our Roger Bacon was born. The fuel they use is not charcoal, but a species of black mineral resembling solid clay. It burns slowly, and afterward the cinders are collected, pounded in a mortar, and made into bricks that can be reburnt. And, do you know, they never employ gold or silver for trading purposes, or indeed metal of any kind. Their currency consists of pieces of rice-paper, about the size of one's hand, beautifully engraven and showing the seal of the emperor. When these become torn or dirty, the owner takes them to the mint, and receives new notes in exchange."

"Have they no gold or silver then?"

"Oh yes, abundance. But they cast it into ingots, and reserve it for state purposes."

"Having heard you so far, my dear Brother, I confess that I am skeptical no longer. I can only hope that, when your account sees the light of day, its readers will be equally credulous."

"Put everything down, and preserve what you have written with care. Because, in years to come, when this land and this people will be better known, everything therein recorded will be verified to the letter. I have lived my life and, with death at my door, I am in no mood for imposing falsehoods upon posterity."

∞

As it happens, posterity has done full justice to the sincerity and accuracy of Friar Odoric's reportings.

In one matter, however, his eyesight plainly led him astray. There are not, and never were, in China tortoises as large as the cupolas of St. Anthony's basilica in Padua. What he saw (from a great distance) was the roof of a temple tiled with tortoise-shell, and so well tiled that it looked like the complete animal.

∞

Lepanto

In the annals of the Christian Church, few dates have more significance than the year 622. It was then that Mahomet made his famous flight — the Hegira — from Mecca to Medina, an incident marking a turning point, not only in his career, but in the larger career of world history. The Prophet began by being a religious reformer, pure and simple; from now on, he assumes the role of political adventurer as well. His project of founding a universal empire was cut short by death, but nothing was able to check the impetuous ambition of those who succeeded him. Within an incredibly short space of time, Syria, Palestine, Mesopotamia, Egypt, North Africa, and Spain had, one by one, become the spoil of Islam.

In this way, it came about that, just when Christians were beginning to have high hopes of the conversion of our continent, they had to stand by and watch this relentless power playing havoc with some of their most treasured acquisitions. And, yet, to say that they stood by would not be a fair description either, because between the years 1096 and 1270, no fewer than eight Crusades were launched against the Mohammedans. These were primarily concerned with the recovering of the Holy Land, and with the maintenance of the Latin colonies in the Middle East; but they had the indirect effect of preventing the enemy from carrying his conquests farther westward.

The Moslems were conquered by the Mongols and Turks in the late Middle Ages, but the victors adopted Mahomet's religion, so that the menace to the faith and independence of Europe became greater than ever. Under Suleiman the Magnificent, the Ottoman Turks reached the zenith of their strength and expansion. When he died, in 1566, he left behind an empire of more than fifty thousand square miles, embracing the richest and most famous regions of the Old World. With the exception of Italy, the Turkish dominions, at that time, comprised all the localities celebrated in biblical and classical history, all the districts that witnessed the beginnings of the Christian apostolate, all the places rendered famous by the journeyings of St. Paul. In Alexandria, Jerusalem, Damascus, Smyrna, Antioch, Athens, Philippi, and on the sites of Memphis, Troy, Carthage, Tyre, Nineveh, Babylon, and Palmyra, the inhabitants obeyed the orders of the Sultan of Constantinople. The Ottoman Crescent stretched from the Atlas to the Caucasus.

The founder of the line was the son of a petty chieftain who ruled over four hundred families in central Asia; but, in the fourteenth century, he crossed the mountain heights separating Christendom from the Mohammedan conquests. This was the beginning of a series of victories, lasting nearly three hundred years, which brought the invaders to the gates of Italy.

In 1354, the Turks stormed and captured Gallipoli, thus obtaining a foothold in Europe for the first time. Seven years later, they occupied Adrianople and made it their European capital. Before the end of the same century, in the battle of Kosovo, they proved themselves more than a match for the combined armies of the Serbians and their Christian allies. Constantinople fell in 1453 and, soon after, Venice was involved in a sixteen-year war, during which she lost many of her Eastern possessions. Another century had hardly passed before Greece forfeited her independence; and, with Rhodes and Tripoli gone, in spite of the valor of the Knights, the Mediterranean was almost out-of-bounds to Christian vessels. For the inhabitants of Tunis, Algiers, and Morocco, the chief source of livelihood was the plunder brought home by their corsairs, augmented by the ransom-money paid over for the thousands of captives they made.

The occupation of Italy, the key to the complete domination of the West, had been determined on by Suleiman; but in the midst of his campaign against Austria, the bursting of a blood vessel suffocated him in his sleep. Still, he lived long enough to witness the emergence of Turkey as a first-class naval power, so that in 1565, a determined, but happily ineffectual, effort was made to take the island of Malta. As for the Ottoman land forces, they were the mightiest and best equipped of any at that time. They were trained to go anywhere, and to do anything, and they relied for their success on the overwhelming weight of artillery they were able to throw into an action. It was in this way that the fate of Cyprus had been sealed, Famagusta alone being battered by 1,500,000 cannonballs. This assault is said to have cost the Turks fifty thousand of their best men, which would seem to show that, in hand-to-hand encounters, the Christians still retained the advantage. But, like the battle of Valmy many years later, the siege of Cyprus was, from first to last, a victory for the guns and gunners.

It was this last disaster that roused the Western nations most nearly concerned to a realization of their common danger. And, indeed, by this time, the Turks were making no secret of their intentions. In the treaties they entered into, now and again, with the Christians, they referred to their Sultan as "The Refuge of Sovereigns," "the Distributor of Crowns to the Kings of the Earth," "the Master of Europe and Asia, the Shadow of God upon the Earth."

Often, to its cost, divided politically, Europe in this crisis was divided on religious grounds as well. In spite of that handicap, the Mediterranean powers made serious efforts and sacrifices, with the result that the combined fleets of Spain, Genoa, and the Papal States mustered at Messina in the early autumn of 1571. Don John of Austria brought a squadron consisting of seventy Spanish galleys, six Maltese, and three from the kingdom of Savoy. The twelve galleys contributed by Pope Pius V were captained by Mark Anthony Colonna, while the Genoese vessels were under the leadership of Andrea Doria, who was destined to fall in the action. Meanwhile, up in the Adriatic, the main part of the Christian armament was being assembled by the Venetian Admiral Veniero, 108 galleys, with six galliasses, or heavy warships, under orders to rendezvous at Corfu. All the ships were manned by picked crews, and they carried an army of twenty thousand good soldiers.

With a view to avoiding those fatal jealousies which were the curse of the Christian powers in nearly all the enterprises they engaged in against the Mohammedans, the Pope himself was appointed head of the League, or director-in-chief of the expedition. He thereupon chose Don John as his supreme lieutenant, and the commandant in charge of the actual operation. News of what was going on soon spread, so that recruits from all over Europe flocked to Messina, eager to serve in such a cause and under so renowned a captain. Among these was the man who was destined to write one of the really great books of the world, Miguel de Cervantes, the author of *Don Quixote*. When he was twenty-one, he left Spain in the company of an Italian cardinal whose service he had entered;

but he had hardly landed in Italy when the drums began to beat for volunteers in the great struggle then impending. They sounded like music in his ears, and he quitted his irksome post and made tracks for Messina. There he encountered, and became a close friend of, one Spiridion Ayoub, an Armenian who had been a high-ranking officer at the court of the Sultan, but had deserted and fled the country to avoid assassination.

In the most flourishing days of the Ottoman power, the great mass of the holders of office were renegades or the sons of renegades. The native Turk was seldom employed at all. The Janizaries, for example, who constituted the Sultan's own bodyguard as well as his standing army, were recruited from the converts to Islam taken from the Rayas, or Christian subjects, of the empire. Spiridion was one of these. As a youth, he had been taken captive and forced to accept, or make a show of accepting, the Mohammedan faith. But he was a Christian at heart, and the first-hand information he had at his disposal concerning the disposition of the Turkish naval forces he now placed at the service of the Catholic League. However, he was by no means optimistic regarding the prospects of the coming battle.

"They tell me," Cervantes was saying, "that the Venetians are bringing into the fight a number of galliasses of two thousand tons' burden, with heavy cannons mounted on them. That ought to be a surprise for our friends the enemy."

"No doubt," replied Spiridion. "But naval battles are not going to be won by means of the carracks you speak of. They are all very well as supply vessels, but the fighting-ships are the galleys. These monsters might be very formidable indeed if you could provide them with a stout gale blowing all the time in their favor; but, in a calm, they need an army of rowers to make them move. And, meantime, the built-up stem and stern of these carracks offer first-class targets to the gunners on the other side. In contrast, the hull of a galley lies low in the water and, besides, it is by common consent the greyhound of the sea. My own opinion is that the coming battle will be won by the side that has the best galleys, and the skill to make the best possible use of them."

"But surely the Venetians have always excelled in the construction of these same galleys?"

"Yes, indeed. But you must remember that Venetian designers and craftsmen have been working in the Turkish dockyards for years. The result is that it is not easy now to tell one galley from another."

The ships in question, which were sometimes 165 feet in length, were furnished at the prow with a boarding-grab painted black, which the Turks nicknamed "the raven." The after-part was occupied by a large poop, or quarterdeck, on which the captain and the soldiers taking part in the action were stationed. The guns were mounted on a narrow platform that ran the whole length of the vessel. The rowing benches were arranged on a gunwale, or gallery, projecting over the ship's side; twenty-six oars to a side, with three and sometimes five men to an oar. They were furnished with a mainmast, or a foremast, carrying lateen sails. These were seldom unfurled in rough water, because the narrowness of the vessel exposed it to the danger of capsizing. But in good weather, or on the smooth surface of the Mediterranean, this galley, in proper hands, was invincible.

"As for me," Cervantes insisted, "I am confident that we shall gain the victory; and it will be a decisive one. You yourself admit that the Turks habitually rely on vain boasts, exaggerations, and falsehoods to keep up the morale of their fighting men. A tactic of that kind may, and perhaps must, succeed once, twice, and again and again. But any lie, even the most successful, is begotten of weakness. And I believe that that weakness of theirs will be their undoing in the long run. These people are not, and do not even believe themselves to be, as formidable as they make out. After all, we lost Rhodes only through an act of treachery."

"You are right there, certainly."

"And look what happened at Vienna, almost in our lifetime. The invincible Suleiman in person, the greatest of all their Sultans, leads a quarter of a million men, supported by three hundred cannons, against a city defended by sixteen thousand, and defended behind a wall only six feet in thickness. The outcome of that siege was deemed inevitable by nearly everyone on our side. Yet, the assailants were compelled to retreat, after losing the flower of their forces. Vienna was saved, thanks to the valor of her defenders."

"Do not forget the Count of Salm who directed the defense. Where shall we find his like again?"

"We have his equal at this moment. There is no better captain alive today than Don John, an Austrian like the Count of Salm. And let us not forget Malta. That bastion of ours had no more than seven hundred knights, and nine thousand soldiers, against a besieging force of thirty-five thousand, led by the Grand Vizier and reinforced by first-rate captains. Yet it sustained ten general assaults, and compelled the aggressors to withdraw after five months. Let us, my brother, arm ourselves with the brave words that La Vallette addressed on that occasion to his men-at-arms: 'A formidable enemy is coming like a thunderstorm upon us; and, if the banner of the Cross must sink before the unbelievers, let us see in this a signal that Heaven demands from us these lives which we have solemnly devoted to its service. He who dies in this cause dies a happy death. Meanwhile, to render ourselves worthy to meet it, let us renew at the altar those vows which ought to make us, not only fearless, but invincible.' "

"There are some among yourselves who recommend a new treaty with the enemy in order to gain time."

"I trust we may not fall into that specious trap. Believe me, there is no alternative; Europe must either fight now or die. The Turks have determined on its conquest. Has not their Sultan but lately boasted that he will not rest until he has foraged his horse on the main altar of St. Peter's in Rome? Of course, they are always willing to make treaties of peace, but that is part of their strategy. We all know what happened to Cyprus. That island they barbarously assaulted and captured, in open violation of the treaty existing between them and Venice; and the commandant Bragadine they flayed alive, in spite of the fact that he surrendered on a solemn promise given that the lives of the garrison would be spared. The last Bosnian king and his sons surrendered to the Sultan, on a written guarantee to the same effect. But the Sultan consulted the Mufti, the keeper of his conscience, and was told that oaths and promises were never binding in the case of Christians. The Mufti even asked, and obtained permission to be the executioner of the king, as a testimony to the sincerity of the moral decision he had given. However, you who have been on the spot must be better acquainted with these criminals than I."

"In all this they are the worthy followers of their accursed prophet, Mahomet. According to the Koran, he considered himself under a religious obligation to fight the unbelievers — that is to say, people like us — until they all cry out, 'There is no God but God.' He adds, 'Only when they pronounce these words will their lives and property be safe from me.' "

"I suppose," said Cervantes, "that any people habituated to conquest and the waging of war will become ruthless. My own ancestors were known to the Romans as people who preferred to kill their captives rather than have them on their hands."

"But the ruthlessness of the Turk is a cold-blooded, calculating thing. It is an attribute and policy of their rulers, great and small. One accepted tradition among them is to the effect that their Sultan has a right, on any given day, to put to death seven men — seven, mind you, no more — without any other excuse save that he is minded to do so. It is strange to hear the people referring to him, in their ordinary conversation, as *Hunkiar*, that is to say, "The Manslayer." They do it quite openly, and look upon the epithet as a high compliment paid to his power of life and death. Did not Suleiman cause all his rightful heirs to be assassinated, at the bidding of Roxana, whose ambition it was to secure the succession to her son Selim, the present Sultan?"

"Well, my hope and my conviction are that the blow, now to be struck, will enable Europe eventually to drive this foul pest forever from her borders."

∞

Lepanto is a small town situated on the coast of Locris in middle Greece. It is the ancient Naupactos, which means "a dockyard," and it gives its name to an arm of the sea connecting the Bay of Patras with the Straits of Corinth. Not so far away is the island of Ithaca, famous as the reputed home of Ulysses. Not so far away is Missolonghi, where Byron died in 1824.

The Turks had invaded the adjacent territory in 1498 and were now using the harbor of Lepanto as a rallying place for their naval forces. These amounted to 240 galleys, with sixty vessels of a smaller size, manned by nearly twenty thousand Christian slaves, chained to the oars and lashed into obedience by the official taskmasters.

Ali Pasha was commander-in-chief, and under him were eighteen Beys, each of whom was entitled to hoist his banner on a galley as a Prince of the Sea. The total personnel amounted to up-wards of sixty thousand.

As soon as the news of the whereabouts of this armada reached the ears of Don John, he decided on the bold venture of attacking it while it was still, more or less, at anchor. He knew that the naval strategy of the Turks was usually planned on the assumption that the initiative would lie with themselves. "They are a superstitious people," he told his subordinates, "a people who firmly believe that things must go a certain way. Let us take advantage of that foi-ble, and give these fatalists a surprise."

Without delay, the order was passed along. Early in October, the Messina flotilla was in full sail for the western coast of Greece, a distance of about three hundred miles as the crow flies. At Corfu, they linked up with the Venetian contingent under Admiral Veniero. By a miracle of good fortune, no hint of the oncoming peril reached the Turks until it was almost at their door.

In the grey dawn of the morning of October 7, people going about their affairs in the district lying at the mouth of the Aspro Potamo were astounded to observe, far out at sea, the dim outline of an immense squadron making all speed for the entrance to the Gulf of Patras. Runners were instantly dispatched to warn the Ot-tomans. They had just time to embark their reinforcements and move out into the gulf after which the coming engagement was to be named. The wind was in their favor, for the time being, and be-fore long, their ships were seen to fan out in the form of a crescent, a sure sign that they intended to give battle.

The Christians lost no time in making their predetermined dis-positions. A division of between fifty and sixty galleys swung into position, on the right and left wings respectively, while Don John threw, into the space between, the heaviest part of his armament. To make it heavier still, he placed his six galliasses at intervals along the front to act as redoubts, or firing-points, more or less stationary. He himself and the other two admirals, each in a separate galley, took up their stations somewhat in advance of the center. On seeing this last move, Ali Pasha chivalrously brought forward his own galley, along with that of his two chiefs, as though to answer the challenge of the Austrian. The Turks threw every ship they had into this formation, with the result that their line stretched from shore to shore, and outflanked that of the Christians. This looked like an advantage, but it was more than counterbalanced by the absence of a reserve, and by the fact that their opponents had one of sixty vessels commanded by the Marquis of Sainte Croix. He was destined to play a decisive part in the campaign.

During that mysterious and spontaneous silence that seems to be the immediate prelude to every great battle, each side regarded, with admiration and awe, the strength and splendor of its adversary's array. While his officers harangued their men, and led them in prayer for victory, Don John unfurled the Gonfalon, or banner, sent by the Pope, on which was embroidered an image of our Savior crucified. On his part, the Turkish admiral fired a gun, charged with powder only, as a signal to begin the action. To the sound of drums and fifes, the main Ottoman squadron rowed forward, with the plain object of forcing a decision by breaking the Christian center. It was here that Veniero's galliasses repaid to the full the trust that had been reposed in them. The destruction their heavy guns wrought was greater than anything hitherto experienced in this kind of warfare. They concentrated their fire on the rowing benches and, as the wind had by this time veered to the east, the oarless galleys of the Turks became sitting targets for the cannonballs.

The two leaders of the opposing fleets encountered each other face to face, and for two hours their vessels fought it out with the

most determined obstinacy. But the death of Ali Pasha who, like Nelson, was shot down by a sniper, decided the contest. His flagship was boarded and taken; and soon after, his whole center disintegrated and fell into utter disorder. True to their habit in defeat, the Turks offered no resistance, so that the combat degenerated into a massacre.

Only on the left wing did the Ottomans have any success. There the Genoese squadron, under Andrea Doria, was assaulted so vigorously that, in the confusion, it parted company with the center. This dangerous situation was retrieved by the prompt action of Sainte Croix, who brought up some of his reserves and closed the gap. As it was, Doria's galley was boarded, and he himself was killed in a hand-to-hand encounter with one of the Turkish commanders. This same commander, seeing that the day was irretrievably lost, collected forty of his best ships, broke through the Christian line, and stood safely out to sea.

These were the only enemy vessels that escaped. Of the rest, ninety-four were sunk, burned, or run aground and destroyed upon the coast. The rest were captured. Thirty thousand Turks were slain. The casualties on the other side were small in proportion, but among them was Cervantes, who, stationed on board the galley *Marquesa*, distinguished himself, and lost the use of one of his hands through a wound from an arquebus, a portable firearm superseded by the musket. To the end of his life, he rejoiced to think he had been present at Lepanto, "on that day, so fortunate for Christendom, when all nations were undeceived of their error in believing that the Turks were invincible at sea."

From that day, indeed, dates the rapid decline of the Turkish empire. On receipt of the news of the calamity, the Sultan neither ate, nor drank, nor showed himself for three days; a heroic sacrifice on the part of the man who earned for himself the nickname of

Christians Courageous

Selim the Sot. Some historians have suggested that, had the allies pushed on to Constantinople immediately after the battle, that city might have fallen into their hands. That is a matter for conjecture. What is certain is that the fight was a turning point in European history, since it averted forever the danger of a Mohammedan invasion of our continent.

There is this besides. The engagement was the end of an epoch in naval warfare. The classic galley of the ancient Greeks and Romans, the long, narrow warship propelled by oars, was the boat that figured in this battle, and figured for the last time as far as any big-scale operation is concerned. Like the Turkish Empire, it, too, received its *coup de grâce* in the Gulf of Lepanto.

∞

Indian Summer

The prospects of converting India to the Christian Faith were probably never brighter than at the beginning of the seventeenth century. That Faith had found a firm footing in the country at a very early stage; tradition would say at the earliest possible stage. When the Portuguese came on the scene in the year 1498, they found communities of native Christians scattered along portions of the Malabar and Coromandel coasts. These people were firmly convinced that their forefathers had been won over to the gospel by no less a person than St. Thomas. In corroboration of their claim, they pointed to the tomb of the apostle, near Madras, which was still held in great veneration and was identified with the site of his martyrdom. In that locality is still to be found a granite bas-relief cross with an inscription to that effect written in ancient Persian.

Yet apart from the historical value of their claim, the communities in question were almost insignificant relative to the population of the country as a whole. The interior of the vast "continent" remained practically untouched, until the sixteenth century was drawing to a close, in spite of the fact that able missionaries such as the Jesuits had, by that time, been on the spot for more than fifty years. Indeed, the obstacles that confined their activities to the coastal fringe appeared, at first glance, to be insurmountable.

In the south, the religious situation was at the mercy of the Brahmins. From time immemorial, the spiritual government of the masses had been in their hands; they decided what the people at large were to believe. They set the religious pace, so to say; and, generally speaking, their culture and integrity were such that they were well qualified to do so. It was obvious that the process of conversion would, in this case, have to start at the very top and work downward. But how was one to set about converting the Brahmins? That was the question which, for years, no one found easy to answer. The caste system made them unapproachable, more especially by Europeans, of whom they had a very poor opinion. They judged Europeans by the samples of them that came across in the persons of the Portuguese settlers, or traders, whose general behavior provided even the missionaries themselves with a permanent headache.

In the north, there was Akbar, the real founder of the Mogul or Mongol Empire, whose sway reached from the mountains of Persia to the borders of Hyderabad. In the end, he was ruling over a greater portion of India than had ever given its allegiance to a single ruler. The splendor of his court was unsurpassed anywhere, and he was waited on by no fewer than twenty vassal kings. He was not only the man of the hour; he was the man of the future. Already he had been awarded the ominous title "Guardian of Mankind"; and, provided he lived long enough, there was no reason he should not make himself master of the entire peninsula, Ceylon included. It was well known that he had big ideas and was planning the unification of the whole country. His broadmindedness and toleration were being talked about in the very streets and bazaars.

And yet, when all was said that could be said, he and his were full-blooded Mohammedans; and, down to date, how many of these could be counted among the trophies of the Christian apostolate? Not only that, but the Mogul was to the Mohammedan world very much what a descendant of the House of Jesse would be to a nation of Jews.

Such was the formidable problem that presented itself, like a two-headed monster, to these missionaries at their first coming into that corner of the Far East. Nevertheless, for one brief and dazzling moment, it seemed as though providence was going to deliver the solution into their eager hands.

Father Robert de Nobili, the Italian Jesuit, came face-to-face with the Brahmin difficulty as soon as he arrived on the Malabar coast in 1606. Having mastered the Tamil language and made himself acquainted with the beliefs and practices of the Hindus of the highest castes, he resolved upon a bold and heroic course. Clothing himself in the dress of a *saniassy*, or ascetic, he made his way into the interior and, after a tedious journey, reached the city of Madura. On being questioned by the authorities, he told them that he was not a Portuguese but a Roman rajah who craved their hospitality in order that he might practice penance, pray, and study the sacred law. On the strength of this declaration — which was true in every particular — he was assigned lodgings in the Brahmin quarter. Before long, he changed his title of rajah for that of Brahmin; and, because of his penitential way of living and his extraordinary familiarity with Indian literature, both sacred and profane, he was taken for a genuine member of that caste. Incidentally, de Nobili was the first European to read and study Sanskrit, the language in which most of the ancient books of India were written, beginning with the oldest parts of the Vedas, dating from about 2000 BC. Having mastered this work, he used its teaching in demonstration of the truths of the Christian Faith. By and by, the priest's time was wholly taken up in granting interviews. He charmed his audience by the ease with which he conversed, and the faculty he displayed in quoting the most famous of their authors. As a diversion, he would recite or sing snatches of the native poetry.

Then began the conversions. In less than two years, he had baptized several of the foremost Brahmins of the city. Nothing succeeds like success; and, eventually, Father de Nobili, with the assistance of some other Jesuits, extended his campaign to the whole interior of southern India. He himself labored in Mysore and the Karnatic, finding time, meanwhile, for the composition of numerous Christian writings in the Sanskrit, Tamil, and Telugu languages. When, at the end of forty years' exertion, old age and complete blindness compelled him to retire, the annual number of conversions amounted to five thousand. At the close of the century, the total number of Christians in the mission-field he had established was 150,000. This was in spite of the fact that there were never more than seven Jesuits engaged in the work, although, of course, they had the services of many native catechists.

∞

So far, so good. Still there was no getting away from Akbar. His was the shadow lying over India at the moment. And so it came about that, although Agra was a thousand miles away, to the missionaries, interest in it turned it into a real next-door neighbor. All the hours they could spare they devoted to the Persian language and literature, and to the study of the Koran, the Mohammedan's bible, comforting themselves, meanwhile, with many a far-fetched vision of the mind. And yet, were they so very far-fetched after all? What was to prevent Asia from going the way

Europe had gone; from having its Holy Roman Empire, with Akbar in the role of Charlemagne, and receiving consecration at the hands of the Pope?

From these daydreams they were awakened to reality by an event that stirred the Portuguese colony to its depths.

On an autumn evening in the year 1579, a mortar fired from the fort of Goa announced to the inhabitants that something of unusual importance was going forward. In due course, it was learned that runners had just reached the city to say that an embassy from the court of the Great Mogul was approaching, bearing messages to the civil and ecclesiastical authorities. Without delay, a magnificent cavalcade was formed, and the envoy and his suite were met at some distance from the city and escorted, at his own request, first to the Viceroy's palace, and next to the Jesuit church, where he took off his shoes and venerated the tomb of St. Francis Xavier. Then he presented a letter addressed to the Superior. It ran as follows:

In the name of the Lord of All! This letter comes from Jalaluddin Muhammad Akbar, by God's appointment King, to the Father-in-Chief of the College of St. Paul at Goa. Know that I am very well disposed toward you. Herewith, I send Abdullah, my ambassador, together with Dominic Perez, my Christian interpreter, with the request that you will send me two of your learned priests, together with the books of your Law, especially the gospel, that I may know that Law and its excellence. For I desire to know it. I urge you, therefore, to allow the priests to join this embassy and to come to me, bringing the books aforesaid. Of this you may be sure, that I shall receive them most courteously, and entertain them most handsomely. When I have learned your Christian Law sufficiently to appreciate its excellence, they may depart at their pleasure. I shall honor them with abundant rewards and with an escort. Let them come in perfect security. I take their defense on myself.

On December 13, the three priests chosen for the mission set out, with Rudolph Acquaviva at their head. They went by sea as far as Surat, and then began their long inland trek, which lasted for nearly six weeks. If their expectations on setting out had been inclined to run high, the information imparted to them on the journey, by Perez the interpreter, was calculated to raise them still farther. By his way of it, Akbar was almost a Christian already.

"He is a Mussulman only in name," Perez insisted. "He has abolished most of the rules and regulations of the Koran. He has a new calendar in which the Flight of Mahomet is ignored, and the months have been given Persian names. He does not like Arabic; and as for beards, which the Koran is so particular about, he can hardly be persuaded to admit a hairy-faced man into his presence."

"Perhaps he is partial to the old religion of India, to Buddhism," Acquaviva suggested.

"Well, if he is, he has a strange way of showing it. His respect for the caste-system is such that he has established schools in which all ranks and classes sit side by side on the benches. Child-marriages he has outlawed altogether, as well as the slaughter of animals for sacrifice. And he is taking extreme measures to put an end to the Suttee; you know, the self-immolation of Hindu widows on the funeral pyre of their husbands. Not so long ago, he chanced to hear that the Rajah of Jodhpur was going to compel his son's widow to sacrifice herself in that way, and Akbar mounted his horse and rode to the spot to prevent it.

"And what is this that one hears of his plan for a united empire, and a kind of catholic, or universal, religion?"

"I can vouch for the truth of that report, at any rate. I have often heard him say that, if the diverse peoples of Asia are to be brought together and taught to live in harmony, it will only be thanks to a religion independent of and superior to all the others."

"But that is just the statesman talking. Is he personally concerned one way or the other? Rumor has it that he is little better than a broadminded atheist."

"I don't believe it. Do you know, he once told me in confidence that, if he felt convinced that God called him to the Catholic Faith, neither his throne, his children, nor his harem would stop him from leaving everything, and going into private life at Goa."

"Well, then, if that is the case, we must make it our business to see that he is convinced. Will he be willing to listen to us — I mean, to listen to the truth as distinct from the usual clap-trap of toadies and flatterers?"

"What he delights in," said Dominic, "are discussions and debates. He loves nothing better than a good argument. He has hundreds of religious teachers at his court, and he sets them disputing, the one against the other; the Mohammedan Mollas and Ulemas against the Hindu Brahmins and Ascetics. If you can get the better of all these disputants — and I have no doubt on that score — that will be half the battle."

"And the other half of the battle — how is that going to be won?" the Jesuit asked with a laugh.

"A miracle would do it, even a small one. These Moguls are very keen on signs and portents. If I were a juggler, or a sorcerer, I could make my fortune at the court. As it is, there are dozens of them there; all doing well, too, I assure you."

"Yes," replied Acquaviva, "my own opinion is that it needs some sort of a miracle to convert any Mussulman, never mind one of their rulers. Tolerant and non-committal this Akbar of yours may appear to be in matters religious, but officially he is God's Caliph, the Defender of the Moslem faith. He is surrounded by these Mollas and Ulemas you speak of. They are the watch-dogs who guard the Moslem faith and practice, the oracles who expound and interpret the laws of the Prophet. Although he would be the last to admit it, you may be sure that, in his secret soul, Akbar is intimidated by the terrible threats the Koran pronounces against all those who forsake the path mapped out by Mahomet."

"There is something in that, I must confess. You know that anyone who enters the presence-chamber is obliged to kiss the ground in front of the emperor. That is one of Akbar's innovations, and the Mollas don't like it one bit. They are always invoking the teaching of the Prophet, who forbade his followers to pay that sort of homage to any earthly ruler, however exalted."

"Yes, and there is the political factor as well. It is all very fine to plan an Asiatic empire, whose discordant elements would be harmonized by means of a religion acceptable to all and sundry; by means of *our* religion, in short. At the same time, Akbar knows that his enemies are numerous, that they are as busy as he is himself making plans, counter-plans. He knows that powerful elements, in India and elsewhere, are watching for the first opportunity to challenge his right to be what he is, and where he is."

All the same, when the missionaries reached Agra, they began to think that Dominic Perez might be right after all. Akbar received them in state, enthroned cross-legged on a platform of which there is a model in the South Kensington Museum. Upon his head he wore a Hindu turban, adorned with precious stones. His robe was of cloth of gold, and, instead of Moslem trousers, he wore the Hindu *dhoti*. As in Babylon and Egypt in olden times, pages stood by with bows and arrows and other arms, in case the monarch desired to use them. Reporters were at hand, with their tablets, ready to take down every word he might condescend to utter.

The greetings were cordial on both sides. A sum of money was set aside for the Jesuits' use, and they, on their part, presented his majesty with a copy of the recently published Polyglot Bible of Cardinal Ximenes, in several volumes, the last of which contained a Hebrew and Chaldaic dictionary, a Hebrew grammar, and a Greek dictionary. The books and the bindings issued from the famous publishing house of Plantin at Antwerp. On these being brought before him, Akbar took off his turban and placed each volume on his head, after which he kissed it reverently.

For a time, everything went smoothly and hopefully. Thursday night of each week was appointed for a public debate, on moral and spiritual subjects, which the emperor initiated. He would raise some question, and then ask the representatives of the different religions to give their answers. One prolonged and acrimonious discussion turned on the life and doctrine of Mahomet, as compared or, rather, contrasted with those of Christ. The candor with which the Jesuits treated the character and teaching of the Prophet was too much for the prejudices of Akbar himself, who was, as Acquaviva had surmised, a real Mohammedan at heart.

Still, the missionaries did not give in without a struggle. Acquaviva returned to Goa, but Jerome Xavier, a nephew of Francis, took his place. It was he who translated the Gospels into Persian, at Akbar's request, as well as compiling a *Life of Christ* in the same tongue. But what gave the monarch most pleasure was a copy of a famous painting of the Blessed Virgin venerated in one of the churches in Rome. This was taken to the palace and shown to the women of the harem. In the year 1600, the Jesuits erected a representation of the birth of our Savior in their church at Agra, which attracted widespread attention. Great pains were taken with this

Crib, which contained artificial singing birds, figures of monkeys spouting water from their eyes and mouths, and images of the Three Wise Men that shed tears. One Christmas, this Crib was open to the public for forty days, and people came to see it at the rate of fourteen thousand a day, many of them carrying off straws from the manger as souvenirs.

Akbar died in 1605, two years after Queen Elizabeth I of England, with whose reign his practically coincided. He was succeeded by his son, Jahangir, who was even more favorably disposed toward the Christian religion than his father had been. He was certainly a great believer in signs and portents, and his court was a rendezvous for the best fakirs that India could produce. The missionaries were always insisting that their system of religion discountenanced superstitious practices of all kinds. Yet, oddly enough, it was this very magic that, in the end, came near to causing the monarch to seek Baptism.

One day the Grand Vizier presented himself before Jahangir, and announced that a Bengali juggler had arrived in the city, and was most anxious that the Conqueror of the World should have an opportunity of testing his powers.

"What powers?" asked his majesty eagerly.

"Well, not exactly his own powers, All Highest. But he is the owner of an ape, and he claims that this ape is the mouthpiece of Allah himself."

"So! And what then?"

"He humbly craves permission to give a demonstration, Your Mightiness."

"Yes, yes! Let him give it now, in the Chamber of the Audience. And let all attend. We shall see what kind of a prophet His Excellency the Ape pretends to be."

When all were assembled, the juggler introduced his confederate, one of those clever tailless monkeys that have been the showman's stand-by from the earliest times. Making a profound salaam, the Bengali told the emperor that he would require to have the names of twelve famous lawgivers written secretly, each on a separate piece of paper. This was soon done by one of the Mollas, his list of names including that of Moses, Ali, Mahomet, and Christ. The folded papers were put into a bag, well shaken, and then presented to the ape. Without a moment's hesitation, it drew out the paper bearing the name of Christ. But Jahangir suspected that the juggler, who knew Persian, might have assisted the ape in some way, and so he went aside with the Molla, and had twelve fresh papers provided, with the twelve names written this time in the secret cypher of the court. But cyphers did not worry the ape, any more than did the Persian language. With infallible instinct, it rummaged among the folded papers and selected the same name as before.

The Molla now began to fuss and fume, protesting that the whole thing was an imposture, and offering to make the test himself. To this the emperor consented, whereupon the crafty Molla prepared twelve more slips with the same names. But when he came to place them in the bag, he kept back the one bearing the name of Christ, concealing it in his hand. The ape searched the bag, and then searched again, but refused to draw out a paper. On being commanded by the emperor to make a selection, the beast tore the papers up in a fury, making unmistakable signs that the name of the Great Lawgiver was not among them. When the emperor asked where it was, the ape sprang at the Molla, and seized him by the hand in which the slip of paper was concealed.

The missionaries made no attempt to exploit this incident, but they were highly amused at the report that ran through the city, that the emperor had gotten possession of an ape that was a genuine Christian.

Christians Courageous

In eastern Asia, the things that happen most easily are the unforeseen, the unexpected things. Jahangir died, as he had lived, a Mohammedan. Before the century was out, his royal house had begun to enter on its dotage. The emperors continued to succeed one another, but their empire ended by being little more than a name. The political history of India has been compared to a succession of tidal waves, the one following close upon the other, and each receding to make room for its successor. The Mogul dynasty was just another of these waves.

Among the Redskins

On a certain April morning, in the year 1615, there was an unusual stir going forward in the newly founded city of Quebec. We say city, although Quebec at that time amounted to little more than a few rough-and-ready wooden buildings grouped about the fort.

Canada is said to have been discovered by John Cabot in 1497. He was an Italian navigator, born near Genoa, but he settled in Bristol and received from our Henry VII a patent, or commission, for the exploration of unknown lands in the eastern, western, and northern seas. In his first expedition, he reached Cape Breton Island and Nova Scotia. Some forty years later, Jacques Cartier of St. Malo sailed into the St. Lawrence and took possession of the country for the King of France. He visited two native settlements, Hochelaga, now Montreal, and Stadacona. It was another Frenchman, Champlain, who founded the present capital on the site of the second of these two villages. Soon after, the work of winning over the native Indians was taken in hand by a small body of Franciscans and Jesuits based on Quebec.

A glance at the map will show how well situated their headquarters were. With a stout canoe, an Indian guide and, perhaps, a fishing-line and a musket, you had all the equipment you needed.

Thanks to the St. Lawrence and its tributaries, you could — barring the hostility of the natives — reach any one of the Great Lakes: Huron, Erie, Michigan, Superior, and Ontario, on the banks of which large populations were encamped.

And now, in the spring of the year in question, Quebec was swarming with Indians. No fewer than forty canoes had traveled hundreds of miles for the annual fur market. Their passengers included a great number of petty chiefs or captains, sixty all told. These were the Wyandottes (after whom the hens are called), whose home at that time was in the territory lying between Georgian Bay and Lake Simcoe, in Ontario. When a few of these first appeared in Quebec, the French noticed that the ridge-like arrangement of their hair resembled the bristles of a wild boar (*huré*) and so they nicknamed them Hurons. One of the Franciscan missionaries then in Quebec, Father Joseph le Caron, had picked up a smattering of their language, and when the day's bartering was over, he was usually to be found around one of the campfires, endeavoring to gain the favor of the braves. He made little or no progress until he chanced to learn that, among the tribesmen there and then assembled, was a young Indian called Hinonskwen, who knew a certain amount of French. After that, things began to look up.

"Tell me, Hinonskwen — this tribe of yours: where is it located?"

"Far away. Many miles away. Maybe a thousand. On the shores of a mighty water."

"And yet you come to Quebec every year."

"Yes, we come to give and to receive. We have fine skins; you have many things we need."

"But how do you come?"

"By water. Nearly all the way by water. There are rivers and rivers; big rivers and small rivers, and there are big pools of water besides, water that does not flow."

"How long does it take?"

"Sometimes four weeks; sometimes more. There are forests in between the rivers. We carry our canoes and skins through the forests, and then we are on a river again."

"How many are there in your tribe?"

"Many; many thousands; perhaps forty thousand."

"And do you live in villages?"

"Yes, in villages; there are eighteen villages in our nation. We do not roam about like the others; we live a quiet life."

This last item of information was most valuable. One big obstacle the missionaries had to contend with arose from the nomadic, or wandering, habits of the Indians. They were always on the move from one hunting ground to another. It was difficult to teach people existing in such a restless condition.

"Would it be possible for me to reach your country?" was the priest's next question.

"Yes, it would be possible. With a good canoe and a good guide."

"Would you be my guide?"

"Yes, I will be your guide."

And so it was arranged there and then. Hinonskwen was to remain behind in Quebec, until such time as the small expeditionary party had made its arrangements. He would undertake to bring them to his nation. A situation hitherto regarded as almost hopeless now began to appear distinctly promising.

Looking at the map of North America — Canada and the United States — we see hardly anything but a huge collection of cities and towns. There are plenty of open spaces, of course, and these spaces are diversified by great lakes and rivers. But the general appearance suggests a teeming urban population, millions congregated mainly in the big industrial centers. It is difficult to realize that all this is a recent development and transformation. Less than three hundred years ago, this immense region was almost unbroken forest, inhabited by those among whom the simplest arts of civilized life were unknown. The Indian tribes were so numerous that nearly every river, lake, and stretch of territory has handed down the name of a distinct nation. Thus, to give but a few instances, among the rivers we have the Arkansas, the Seneca, the Illinois; among the lakes, the Huron, the Erie, and the Oneida; and, among the districts, Assiniboia, Ottawa, and Delaware.

These people were called Redskins, but in fact, their faces were not naturally red at all but brown. In some cases the color was almost yellow. When Columbus landed on the island of Española in 1492, he found himself in the midst of these same brown-skinned people, and this confirmed him in the belief that he had reached India. He called these brown-skins Indians, and the name has stuck to them ever since. Later exploration showed that this same brown-skinned race was spread over the whole continent, from the Arctic to Cape Horn, the Eskimos excepted. But the natives in the north were fond of using paint, especially red paint.

The missionaries had unusual difficulties to contend with. There was first of all the size of the territory; Canada alone has an area of nearly four million square miles. Then, as has been said, there were the roving propensities of the natives; you might reach their village, only to find that the men had gone to the hunting grounds and were not expected back for months. But the biggest problem of all was the language; and not one language, but upward of two hundred, to say nothing of a perfect welter of minor dialects. And, since the Indians did not possess any literature, every single word you heard had to be written down on paper, in letters corresponding to the sound.

Here, at last, however, was an opportunity of making a start with a nation, friendly, stay-at-home, and accessible. Father le Caron decided to throw in his lot with the Hurons, to live among them, share their life, and master their language. From this beginning, who knew what big results might one day be forthcoming?

When the time drew near for the great adventure, Hinonskwen himself selected the canoe, a strong, well-knit craft that had seen good service, and one that could be carried or dragged overland without serious difficulty. Apart from a small chest, there was hardly any baggage at all. The guide made it clear that they could live quite well on the pickings to be had on the way; wild Indian corn, herbs, and pulses, besides fish and game in plenty that were there for the taking. It was the dry season, and they could depend on reaching their destination before the winter set in. Yet, small though the chest was, it contained articles that were, from the priest's point of view, quite indispensable: sacerdotal vestments, the altar stone for Mass, and certain service books. There was also a good supply of small knives, combs, little bells, fishing-hooks, needles, thread, and other trifles as presents for the Indians. Twelve traders from Quebec were to follow in their own canoes at some distance behind.

With the first peep of dawn, on the day appointed, the canoe with its complement of passengers, the priest, Hinonskwen the guide, and a native servant called Tehoronhiongo, was pushed out on to the waters of the St. Lawrence; not far out, however, because the plan was to hug the shore all the way, and thus avoid the current. There was this further advantage: that, in case of disaster overtaking their craft, its occupants might be able to make for the safety of the bank. Hinonskwen, throughout, stuck to the front of the vessel, from which point of vantage his practiced eye could detect danger long before it came near. Concealed rocks, whirlpools, and the endless succession of rapids he negotiated by means of a few lightning strokes of the paddles.

Roughly the itinerary was this: up the St. Lawrence, and around the bend to the right, where Montreal now stands, and so on to the Ottawa River, as far as the vicinity of Lake Nipissing, then due west across this lake to the source of the French River, which quickly carried them to the placid waters of Lake Huron; all told, a matter of seven hundred miles, maybe, allowance being made for the unavoidable detours. This was called the trail-and-water route. There was water practically all the way, with the exception of a strip of forest, at the end, which they had to traverse, sometimes dragging, sometimes carrying, the baggage and the canoe. There were plenty of what the French called *saults* — that is to say, rapids or falls — but thanks to the guide, they were able to shoot most of these without much trouble. But in places where they were too dangerous, there was nothing for it but to land, and work their way along the bank, until the danger-spot was bypassed.

Fortunately the banks of the St. Lawrence were then peopled by Algonquins, who were allies of the Hurons. But there was always the risk of treachery, on the part of this or that straying member of the Iroquois tribe. Consequently, whenever they went ashore to eat or to sleep, Hinonskwen and Tehoronhiongo did sentry duty, turn about. And good sentries they were, with ears alert to the slightest sound, and eyes that could distinguish objects at an immense distance. The Redskins might look all alike to a stranger, but they themselves could recognize the member of another tribe by the faintest streak of paint, or the slightest variation in the arrangement of his feathers.

Arrived at their destination, Hinonskwen, the guide, bade the Fathers wait while he went off to bespeak the goodwill of the chief, Skandegorhaksen. With that, he disappeared into the forest. In due course, he returned to say that the coast was clear and that the chief would grant the missionary an interview. This took place in a clearing away from the wigwams, with twelve of the braves forming a circle, the leader being seated in the middle. The open air was always chosen for a pow-wow, as often as there was reason to suspect the presence of spells or enchantments. After a long silence, the chief rapped out a few short sentences, to which his lieutenants replied with grunts and nods. Then the priest was summoned and told to draw near. Lighting his calumet, the chief took a few puffs and passed it to the missionary. Then a wampum, or belt of beads, having been produced, was formally handed over to the stranger. These formalities signified that a covenant of peace had been entered into and solemnly sealed. The proceedings ended with the set formula addressed to the twelve: "See to this matter, for you are the masters here."

An Indian village was a collection of cabins standing side by side to form regular streets. This one, whose name was Carragouha, was surrounded by a palisade forty feet in height, and boasted eighty cabins. The cabins varied in size, and were distinguished by the number of fires they contained. A one-fire cabin housed two families, a five-fire one as many as ten; while, for the needs of twenty-four families, accommodated in a building 150 feet long, there might be two dozen fires. "A tribe of so many fires" — that was how the Redskins reckoned, just as, at one time, calculations were based on the number of hearths.

Immediately, on a signal being given, the whole village was in agitation. A band of women, with axes in their hands, and led by the chief's wife, Gannensagwas, went into the forest and, in an incredibly short space of time, appeared with the entire framework of a wigwam cut and ready for use. This framework consisted of thirty long poles or stakes. The men, meanwhile, had cleared the site — a huge ring excavated in the snow to a depth of four feet, leaving two walls of snow on each side to keep the poles in position. The poles were then bedded in the ramparts of snow, and sloped in such a way that they all met at the top. Rolls of sewn bark were now fetched from the women's quarters, and these were laid upon and fastened to the poles to form a roof. Snow was packed into the spaces at the base of the poles, and then drenched with water. Before long, and thanks to the frost, the structure was as solid as a rock.

Although the "treaty" recently ratified by means of the calumet and the wampum stipulated for a separate apartment, the Indians did not know the meaning of the word *privacy*. The priest, therefore, was liable to have his eight-feet-by-four wigwam invaded almost at any hour of the day or night. In spite of this handicap and of others even more formidable, he was able to perform his religious duties. Greatest wonder of all, he was able to compile a rudimentary dictionary of the Huron-Iroquois tongue. This latter project was really the inspiration and motive of the whole expedition. Until the language difficulty had been overcome, the missionaries could hope to accomplish little. But the Huron-Iroquois speech was a real mother-tongue, since these nations were the original stock whence came a number of separate tribes, access to whom the mastery of that one language would practically ensure.

∞

The making of a dictionary is a long and difficult undertaking at the best of times. As a rule, a number of learned men get together to form a panel, and to each is assigned a portion of the work. The early continental dictionaries were compiled in this way. France produced a standard work, in the eighteenth century, that needed the combined efforts of forty scholars and took forty years. Doctor Samuel Johnson took seven years; and, although he had some assistance, he could fairly claim that the book was his own. None of these dictionaries are mere glossaries, or books of words. As the years pass, the scope of such compositions becomes enlarged to the dimensions of an encyclopedia. There is, therefore, no comparison between a modern dictionary and, say, the lexicon compiled in Alexandria, by Apollonius, in the reign of the Emperor Augustus. He is usually described as the Father of Lexicography; and, no matter how concise his book may have been, he can never be deprived of the credit belonging to the pioneer. Perhaps the greatest, in any line, is the person who makes the first attempt.

On that score alone, Father le Caron's effort deserves to rank as one of the most courageous literary enterprises ever undertaken. To begin with, he was without assistance of any kind. Apollonius had before him the treatises of the grammarians, as well as all the treasures of Greek and Roman literature. Even Doctor Johnson was indebted to a previous work, compiled by Nathan Bailey, just as Bailey himself made use of the services of four smaller and earlier productions. But we have to remember that the whole of the North American continent did not, at that date, contain a scrap of written material; the Redskins possessed no documents of any kind. It is known that Jacques Cartier made a vocabulary of 160 Indian words, but most of these would be useless for religious purposes.

There is this besides. Unlike Apollonius, Johnson, and the others, this missionary was wrestling with a foreign language, and with one of the most foreign of all foreign languages. If you are fairly good at Latin, you can make something of the languages derived from it — Italian, French, Spanish, and so on. If you have to tackle German or Dutch, you get away to a fairly good start. But the Indian dialects conveyed nothing whatever to the eye or ear of the European. This can be seen from the specimen given of the Lord's Prayer, as Father le Caron's hosts would have recited it:

Onaistan de aronhiaè istarè. Sasen tehondachiendaterè sachien-daoüan. Out aiton sa cheouandiosta endindè. Out aioton senchien, ohoüent soone aché toti ioti Aronhiaone. Ataindataia sen nonenda tara cha ecantate Aoüantehan. Onta taoüandionrhens, sen atonarrihoüanderacoiii, to chienne ioti nendi onsa onendionrhens de oüa onkirrihowanderai. Enon ché chana atakhionindahas d'oucaota. Ca senti ioti.

Here was a form of speech whose structure and genius were totally different from any discovered hitherto. There was no room in it for abstract or general ideas; it dealt only with the concrete and the present time. And the verb dominated everything; nouns, adjectives, pronouns — all were conjugated with the verb. One single letter, or the merest whisper of an accentuation, could radically alter the meaning of a whole phrase. And although this, that, and the other dialect might be members of the same family, like some members of the same family their features were so dissimilar that it was not easy to believe that they were kith and kin. Here, for instance, are nine variations of the Amen, or So-be-it:

Huron:	*Ca senti ioti*
Assiniboin:	*Eetchees*
Blackfoot:	*Kamoemanigtoep*
Flathead:	*Komieet zegail*
Osages:	*Ekongtziow*
Menomonee:	*Nhanshenikateshekin*
Pottawotamie:	*Ape iw nomikug*
Ottawa:	*Apeingi*
Chippeway:	*Migeing*

Among the Redskins

As for the environment in which the work was done, just as we can make a picture of Johnson sitting at his table in the upper room of his house in Gough Square, away from the noises of Fleet Street, so, thanks to an account of life in a wigwam written later, by a Jesuit, we can visualize the background against which Father le Caron labored at his task.

The low roof [says the Jesuit aforesaid] prevents you from standing up, so that, when inside, you have to adopt the usual posture of the savages, lying or sitting on the floor. This prison has four discomforts: cold, heat, smoke, and dogs. You have the snow at your head, with only a pine branch between, and the winds are free to enter at a thousand points. Nevertheless, the cold did not annoy me as much as the heat from the fire, which sometimes roasted and broiled me on all sides, for the cabin was so narrow that there was no escape from the fire. As to the smoke, that is a positive martyrdom. It nearly killed me, and made me shed tears all the time, although I had neither grief nor sadness in my heart. I sometimes thought I was going blind, my eyes burned like fire and distilled drops like an alembic. I repeated the psalms of my Breviary as best I could, knowing them half by heart, and waited until the pain might relax a little to recite the lessons; but, when I came to read them, they seemed written in letters of fire or of scarlet. As to the dogs, I do not know that I ought to blame them, for they have sometimes rendered me good service. These poor beasts, not being able to live out of doors, came and lay down sometimes upon my shoulders, sometimes upon my feet: and, as I had only one blanket to serve both as a covering and mattress, I was not sorry for their protection,

willingly restoring to them part of the heat which I drew
from them.

The wigwams admitted hardly any light, so that all the writing
had to be done sprawling on the ground, close to the fire. At first,
le Caron tried to use candles made from rolls of bark, but these
burned out too quickly to be of any use. Meanwhile, he had to sustain life on a diet of sagamity (porridge made of crushed Indian
corn), boiled peas, wild onions, and the fruit of the askutasquash,
which was a kind of gourd. As often as he fell sick, he drank a "sov-
ereign remedy" in the shape of the juice of the maple tree, ex-
tracted by making an incision in the bark. There was no scarcity of
fresh water, for a spring flowed past the door of the wigwam. He
and his fellow-boarders, the dogs, dined and supped with no other
table or chair except the earthen floor.

Our dictionary-maker was a Frenchman by birth, and one of
the first of a heroic band of Frenchmen who endured incredible
dangers and hardships in the service of the Red Indians, the Hurons in particular; services that resulted in the conversion to
Christianity of the whole of that important tribe. And when these
same Hurons became involved in a prolonged and losing war
against their inveterate enemies, the Iroquois, the missionaries
stood by their new converts and eight of their number, six priests
and two lay-brothers, were put to death under circumstances more
revolting than anything to be found in the annals of the early
Church.

It was certainly through no fault of his own that Father Joseph
le Caron was not among these martyrs of North America. Having
returned to France on business connected with the missions, this
man, who had risked his life more than once, succumbed to the
plague at the age of forty-three.

∞

On the Roof of the World

"I assure you, it is so. I was born in Tibet and I lived there until I was twenty. Tibet, I tell you, is practically a Christian country as it is. There's a ripe fruit ready to fall into your hands, and you won't take the trouble to collect it."

The speaker was a certain Tchoking, who, as a youth, had served his apprenticeship in a Lamaist monastery situated on the edge of Lake Manasarowar, near which the Brahmaputra takes its rise. In consequence of some upheaval, he had quitted his community and his country at one and the same time. Crossing over into India, he assumed the garb and way of living of a Hindu ascetic, until, falling in with some Jesuit missionaries, he had eventually gone over to the Christian Faith. Enrolled as a catechist at Agra, he was now busy urging one of the priests stationed there, a Portuguese named Anthony Andrada, to establish a missionary center in his native land.

"I myself," he insisted, "will be your guide and your interpreter." And then he added, "We shall not have far to go, because the king and court are at Tsaparong, on the other side of the hills there."

Tchoking's reference to the hills and the wave of the hand accompanying it set Father Anthony laughing.

"My friend," he said, "by these hills you mean, no doubt, the Himalayas. If they are hills, I should like to know what your idea of a mountain is. As for your suggestion that a few words of instruction will be sufficient to Christianize Tibet, I have been lately hearing very much the same tale about India. But are you aware that it took more than a thousand years to make Europe even nominally Christian? What makes you think that Tibet would be easy?"

"Because, first of all, it is, in its way, the most religious country in the world. Religion shines over Tibet like the light of the sun. And, then, as far as the shape and appearance of this religion go, you might be in your own Portugal, or even in Italy."

"Surely you are joking!"

"No, I am speaking the truth. Tibet is what your ancient Israel was, a theocracy. Of course there is a king at Tsaparong, and there are petty chiefs in other places. But the real ruler of the country is the Grand Lama. If you ask a Tibetan who the Grand Lama is, he has the answer by heart:

> *Behold the King of Kings.*
> *Whose power is as thunder, his thoughts as the sun.*
> *His tongue is a sword, and his words a tempest.*
> *Our hands, our feet, our eyes, our lives,*
> *All must be given up at his command.*

"And his delegates or proxies cover the land. Do you know that something like one-quarter of the male population enters the ranks of the priesthood? I myself once witnessed the funeral procession of a high dignitary, in which over one hundred thousand priests took part. Wherever you go, you find monasteries, with the inmates devoting themselves to study and prayer, just as your monks do in Europe. I tell you, Tibet is a land of prayer."

"Yes, but it is mechanical prayer, by all accounts. I have heard of these Praying-Wheels of yours. You just write a little formula on a narrow strip of paper, and fasten the paper to your wheel, or windmill, whatever it is. That sort of prayer never ceases, by day or by night; except when the wind dies away, which it never does, apparently, at that altitude."

"Oh yes, you will find plenty of superstition in my country, of course; and plenty of the formalism you refer to. But that is not the whole of the story, by any means. As I told you before, the most venerable spot in eastern Asia is the mountain of Buddha near Lhasa. It has been a sacred place since the seventh century. Well, each evening, when the sun begins to set behind the mountain, Lhasa becomes a City of Silence. All work ceases, the noises of daily life are hushed, and the whole population prostrates itself in prayer. As for the Korlos, or Praying-Wheels, even these, I feel sure, began with a sound enough intention. The idea was that you could go about your work, or retire to rest, knowing that your prayer would repeat itself at every turn of the wheel. The crudity of the thing is obvious, but as a symbol, it is significant of a deep-seated belief in the necessity of communication between the two worlds — an uninterrupted communication."

"There may be something in that."

"At any rate, you are mistaken in thinking that our people are lazy, or unwilling to take trouble over their beliefs. It is quite otherwise. There are many shrines among them, places made sacred by the presence of some saintly hermit, maybe, or some inspired oracle. To these, pilgrimages are going on all the time, and the pilgrimage is often a most self-sacrificing business."

"How so?"

"Because it is made, not on foot, nor even on one's knees, but by means of prostrations. The pilgrim starts off by lying prone upon his face, and marking the ground where his forehead rests. He then rises, sets his toes against the mark, and makes a second prostration. In this way, he gets to his destination at last, but it may take him several years."

"And what makes you think that Tibet has been, as you say, half-Christianized already? We have no record of that in Europe, as far as I am aware."

"Well, its religious organization is, in many ways, identical with that of your own Church. There is a real hierarchy, or graduated body of spiritual rulers, with the Grand Lama at its head. These officials carry the crozier and wear the dalmatic, the mitre, and the cope. The clergy chant a sort of office in choir; they practice exorcisms, and bless the people with the right hand, just as you do. In their worship, they use elaborate ceremonial, gorgeous vestments, incense, holy water, beads, litanies, and processions."

"But, my dear Tchoking, we Christians do not claim to have invented all the forms and properties you speak of. Incense was used for religious purposes by the ancient Egyptians and Babylonians, not to mention the Jews. As for counting prayers by means of beads, you Orientals were doing that long before you had any contact with the West. We do not claim a Christian origin for these things, any more than for some of our ceremonial garments, such as the dalmatic, the mitre, the cope, and so on. Even the pastoral-staff was used in pre-Christian times."

"But, then, there is the tradition among the Lamas."

"What tradition?"

"Well, you know that the form of Buddhism peculiar to Tibet was introduced, around about the middle of the fourteenth century, by Tsong-K'apa the Reformer. Now the Lamas insist that this Tsong-K'apa was himself a disciple of a Christian priest, who found his way into the country in the same century. He came from the far west, and had the same sort of face as the Portuguese and French; his nose was prominent, and his eyes sparkled with unearthly fire. For a time, he dwelt in the tent of Tsong-K'apa, and instructed him in the things of Heaven and in the doctrine of the Holy Men of the West. Then, one day he climbed to the top of a mountain, laid his head upon a stone, and slept, never to waken again. But straightway, Tsong-K'apa, his disciple, believing himself to be entrusted with a mission from the God of the Christians, began to travel through the land, preaching and exhorting. And his sanctity and eloquence were such that rulers and people alike embraced many of his ideas. These, in due course, were grafted on the withered stem of the native Buddhism. That is the tale the Lamas tell. It is passed down from one to the other, and committed to memory, like a pedigree or piece of domestic history."

All this, falling upon the ear of Father Anthony Andrada, was like so much seed alighting upon fertile soil. The spirit of adventure was strong in him, and he had more than a fair share of curiosity. And, apart altogether from what might prove to be Tchoking's fairytale, here was a country twice the size of France; and yet, as far as was known, no missionary — no European, in fact — had ever set foot across its threshold. Besides, fairytale or no fairytale, there was no doubt whatever that this unexplored region occupied a strategic position where religion was concerned. It was the headquarters of a worship embracing a far larger portion of the human race than any other pagan superstition. To reach Tibet was to penetrate to the very heart of the Buddhist world. To convert it might result in the automatic conversion of a larger portion of the Asiatic continent.

And so it was there and then decided to make the attempt.

The obstacles to be overcome were formidable enough in all conscience. In olden times, among the primitive Greeks, Olympus, the All-Bright or Peerless — so called because the sun ever shone on its peak — was believed to be the abode of the gods. This mountain, situated in the Vale of Thessaly on the border of Macedonia, is nearly ten thousand feet high. Homer describes its summit as being untroubled by winds or rain, and always girt about with a radiant splendor. Here dwelt Zeus himself. A little lower down, among the ravines and precipices, were the subordinate divinities.

Tibet has every right to be called the Olympus of the Far East. To begin with, it is a mountain in itself, a gigantic tableland, 460 thousand square miles in extent, whose height varies between thirteen and sixteen thousand feet. It is from this tableland, the most massive protuberance on the face of the earth, that the country derives its name. Tibet is *the* plateau, the world's rooftop. The capital stands on a pedestal of its own, over two miles above the level of the sea. And, besides, from time immemorial, this territory, lying between the Himalayas, the Great Wall of China, and the border of Asiatic Russia, has been known as the Staircase of Heaven and the Sojourn of the Immortals; a region that Chinese and Indians alike discussed more or less in whispers. Did not everybody know that Shiva dwelt on one of the highest peaks of the Himalayas — Shiva who carries the source of the Sacred Ganges balanced on his head! And was not that other mighty river issuing out of Tibet, the Brahmaputra — the very offspring of the god Brahma, who made a channel for it by cleaving the rocks with his axe? As for Lhasa, the Throne of God and the Eternal Sanctuary, this ancient city dating from the seventh century has been for a long time the home of the Dalai Lama Vajradhava, the Universal or All-Embracing Lama, the one who, like Jupiter, wields the thunderbolts. He is reputed to be the reincarnation of the sacred ancestor of the Tibetans. Calm and imperturbable, like Tibet itself, he lives out his term of earthly existence, surrounded by a retinue of supporters and saints known as living Buddhas.

Is there any evidence that Mount Olympus was ever scaled, in days gone by, when its reputation subsisted in full vigor? Maybe there is. But it is unlikely that many ventured to disturb that celestial fastness, which poets and peasants represented as being inaccessible to mere mortals. Tibet has enjoyed a similar immunity. Of all the mighty conquerors of the Middle Ages, Kublai Khan alone is supposed to have successfully challenged its splendid isolation.

And, as though religious awe were not barrier enough, there are the physical features of the country itself, and more especially of its approaches. Tibet rises like a citadel in the center of Asia and can defend itself against all corners simply by being Tibet. Its mountains are disposed in such a way as to form a rampart very nearly encircling the whole territory; the Himalayas, for example, which block the route from India, and whose highest peak has only recently been climbed. As one missionary put it, "The Himalayas are not a chain but a world of mountains; to get an idea of what they are like, you would have to soar above them in a balloon."

∞

In the spring of the year 1624, the party was made up. Father Andrada and one companion, accompanied by Tchoking, set out from Agra and, going north to Delhi, attached themselves to a caravan of devout Buddhists who were making a pilgrimage to a shrine on the northern extremity of Nepal. They approached the confines of Tibet by way of the valley running between Nanda Devi and Mount Himla, twin monsters whose combined height amounts to nearly fifty thousand feet. At the end of this valley, they had to reckon with the great barrier of the Snow Abode — that is to say, the aforesaid Himalayas.

Christians Courageous

All the physical obstacles, such as explorers everywhere are accustomed to look for, are here so intensified as to strike terror into the stoutest heart. The main passes connecting the two countries ascend to a height of sixteen thousand feet above the level of the sea. And the track itself is so narrow in places that the traveler has to put one foot before the other, like a man walking the tightrope. To make matters worse, at certain times of the year, one has to reckon with the avalanches. The changing temperature causes huge masses of stone to detach themselves from the mountainside without any warning, and to sweep everything before them, including the track itself.

On reaching certain danger spots, Tchoking would impose strict silence on the party, in the well-founded belief that a sudden guffaw of laughter, or the raising of a single voice, might tip the scale and bring disaster. As it was, the footing in the causeway was so precarious that a thoughtless movement or a momentary inadvertence might send you hurtling to your death in the ravine a couple of miles below.

"For a long way," Father Andrada writes, "we had to go, first on one side, and then on the other, clinging to the boulders with our hands, since a single false step would have resulted in our being dashed to pieces. Added to the terror was the noise made by the rivers, the enormous volume of whose waters, pouring through the clefts in the rocks, created an uproar that the echoes magnified to a frightful degree."

Again and again the track ended abruptly on the edge of a chasm that they had to cross in single file, and by means of the merest wisp of a bridge made of rattan-cane, or bamboo sticks. There was nothing for it here but to close your eyes, get down on all fours, and trust to good fortune. When at last they reached a bit of open country, new hardships presented themselves.

"Sometimes," the account goes on, "we were up to our waists in snow, sometimes up to our shoulders, and never less than knee-deep. There were places, in fact, where we could make progress only by dragging ourselves at full length along the frozen surface, as if we were swimming. Such were the labors of the day, and the night brought us little rest. We spread our cloaks upon the ice, and covered ourselves as well as we could; but, very frequently, the snow fell so thick upon us that we were obliged to rise and shake it off to prevent ourselves from being smothered in our sleep. The cold was so severe that we lost all feeling in various parts of the body, principally the hands, feet, and face. We came near to losing our eyesight as well, and for five and twenty days, I could not read a letter of my breviary."

On arrival, the missionary found the court and the people most friendly, and very eager to hear what he had to say. Nowhere in the world, probably, were the rules of politeness more detailed, or more generally observed. At every hand's turn, you could see people rubbing noses, and saluting one another by scratching the right ear. From the king, the priest received the following concessions:

> We, having felt great pleasure in the arrival of Father An-
> thony Andrada, a Portuguese, to impart the holy law in our
> dominions, grant him perfect liberty to preach and to teach.
> We command, moreover, that a piece of ground be given to
> him whereon to build a church. We, furthermore, most ear-
> nestly solicit the Grand Provincial of the Indies to send the
> said Father Andrada again, that he may instruct our sub-
> jects. Given at Tsaparang and sealed with our arms.

Father Anthony appears to have spent only a short time among the Tibetans; but his achievement, besides being notable in itself, was productive of very valuable results. If we set aside the somewhat shadowy claim of the Polish Dominican Hyacinth, and the less shadowy, but disputed, claim of the Italian Franciscan Odoric, then these two Jesuits were the first Europeans, and the first Christian missionaries, ever to enter this mysterious country. Later on, Andrada wrote a full account of his experiences, and this document supplied Europeans with their first real information concerning Tibet and its inhabitants.

His observations cleared up, for all time, the point about which there had been so much debate and conjecture. These people were not and never had been Christians, but, quite early on, they had managed to assimilate a number of Christian ideas and forms. It is now known that certain Persian Christians, called Nestorians, found their way into China, in the first half of the seventh century, that they were well received, and that their religious enterprises flourished right on until the end of the Mongol period of Chinese history. No doubt it was through contact with these Persian missionaries that the Buddhism of Tibet came to acquire a Christian style and appearance. It is not altogether improbable that the mysterious Man from the West, "having the same sort of face as the Portuguese and the French," at whose feet the revivalist Tsong-K'apa sat as a disciple, was one of these Nestorians.

All subsequent attempts to establish Christianity in Tibet have met with but temporary success. In the same century, the Jesuit Fathers Grueber and d'Orville entered the country by the Sin-ing Road from China, and stayed in Lhasa two months. Later, we hear tell of certain other missionaries contriving to maintain their footing for years, in one case for something like thirty years. Then came the era of European expansion and exploitation in the Far East, with the consequent dropping of a kind of iron curtain by the suspicious Tibetans. A strict watch began to be kept on all the passes, the defiles were guarded by forts, and would-be explorers were arrested, sometimes soundly thrashed, and then escorted to the frontier. Indeed, the number of Europeans who, during the period 1680 to 1880, succeeded in penetrating to the interior of the country can be counted on the fingers of one hand.

Meanwhile, recent events in the Far East have made it only too plain that, as far as the preaching of the gospel is concerned, Tibet is as inaccessible as ever.

∞

Kamiano

Molokai is one of the Hawaiian group of islands that Captain Cook rediscovered in 1778 and christened after the Earl of Sandwich. In appearance it resembles Crete, and in area is almost identical with the Isle of Man.

Here, in the spring of the year 1885, a middle-aged European, barefoot and dressed in a cassock, was standing before a mirror, anxiously studying his features. He was the sole occupant of a small hut whose front windows looked out over the waters of the North Pacific. Although he was a priest and a missionary, well used to roughing it, he was plainly concerned about the appearance of these same features of his. He had good reason for being so, as it turned out. There was something seriously amiss — that suspicion had been hovering around for some months now; but, so far, he had not permitted the suspicion to take possession of his conscious mind.

For years, it had been a habit with him to watch the sun rising over the archipelago — a furtive, stealthy process, he had noticed, leaving a query behind. Who could say just when the night had ended and the day had begun? Such had been the onset of this ailment of his. There had been lassitude at first, a loss of appetite, nausea, neuralgic pains, and an unaccountable feeling of anxiety; one symptom dissolving into another like the colors in the sky at dawn. Then there had been those intermittent fevers, and that subsequent hoarseness and shortness of breath, so embarrassing to one who had to do a fair amount of talking, inside the church and out of it. But with all these premonitions he had steadily refused to parley; in each case, he just hung up the receiver of his attention and turned away.

Now, however, there was this accident of a few moments ago. He had risen as usual, thrown his cassock about him, and set the kettle containing his shaving-water on the stove. He was just preparing to begin, when a thoughtless movement of his hand sent the boiling contents splashing over one of his naked feet. It was an ugly burn and was going to leave an ugly blister behind. But neither at the time nor since had he felt any pain. And yet his feet were healthy enough to look at. This was a disturbing phenomenon, and it had sent him to the mirror, where he was now busy examining those copper-colored blotches, red at first and then brown with a white halo round them. They had been coming and going for some time, the smallest of them about the size of a Belgian franc piece. His left cheek was affected, and there seemed to be something wrong with his left ear; both had a lumpy appearance. There was no room for self-deception here; even the pathetic expedient of postponing the moment of reckoning was no longer tenable.

Oh yes, he knew all about it, knew this disease as few knew it at that date. He had been living with it for nearly twelve years, the only sound individual in a large community of infected men, women, and children. He knew, too, what the sequence was going to be. There was no cure for this complaint. He, who had witnessed the deadly corrosion at work on hundreds of victims, would now experience it at the closest possible quarters. His nails would harden; that thickening of his left cheek and ear would spread to his nose and lips; the hair of his head and eyebrows would begin to fall out. After that, fingers and toes would drop off, joint by joint, painlessly and leaving a well-healed stump behind. There might be ulcers, as well, and running sores, and, if you did not keep a sharp lookout, wounds alive with maggots. "Death before death," that was how the Egyptians described this horror some three thousand years ago. "The firstborn of death," Job called it; and, by all accounts, he knew from actual experience. The feeling that he was now in the grasp of a malady that would, rapidly and of necessity, prove mortal, was like that of a person buried alive or locked up in a burning house.

Snatches of what he had read, with academic curiosity, in his student days returned, like those muffled rumbles of thunder that often came down from the distant mountain.

"The man in whose skin or flesh shall arise a different color or a blister, or, as it were, something shining — that is the stroke of the leprosy . . . And it shall be judged an inveterate leprosy and grown into the skin . . . Then he shall be defiled and shall be reckoned among the unclean . . . He shall have his clothes hanging loose, his head bare, his mouth covered with a cloth and he shall cry out that he is defiled and unclean, and he shall dwell alone without the camp.

"And Giezi went out, a leper white as snow.

"There met Him ten men who were lepers, who lifted up their voice saying: Jesus, Master, have mercy on us."

His next thought was for his flock, more than eight hundred natives in all the stages of a pestilence for which there was no known remedy — hardly even a palliative. Absentmindedly he picked up the jeweled insignia of the Royal Order of Kalakaua,

given to him by Queen Liliukalani herself, in recognition of what
he had done, and was doing, for her stricken subjects. "For their
sakes, I must not lose my nerve. In fact, I must keep my own counsel
until the doctor pays his visit. Fortunately he is due any day now."

He crossed the room and threw open the back window. In the
distance lay the great rampart of Mount Olakui, its dark shadow
falling athwart the settlement, a grim symbol enough of the
shadow resting, at that moment, on his own soul. On his soul? No,
that need not, that must not be. God would see to it. And so he
went on his knees.

∞

One of the paradoxes of leprosy was that more, and yet less, was
known about it than about any other disease. It is almost as old as
recorded history; which means, of course, that it is far older. Like
so much besides, it is supposed to have originated in Egypt. The
Greek physician Hippocrates maintains that it was carried back
from Egypt to Syria by the Phoenician traders. In the history of
Egypt, written by Manetho about two and a half centuries before
the Christian era, it is plainly stated that Pharaoh allowed the Isra-
elites to make their exodus because ninety thousand of them were
lepers. How seriously the Jews were compelled to take the thing,
after crossing the Red Sea, can be gathered from the legislation
drawn up by Moses and set out in the book of Leviticus.

Among the ancients generally, leprosy and the skin complaints
mistaken for it were looked upon as punishments directly inflicted
on the victim by divine justice. The leper was not only defiled; he
was under a curse. As such, he was to shun and be shunned. Even
rulers were not exempted from this ostracism. King Azarias, and
after him King Ozias, as soon as the disease appeared upon them,
abdicated and lived henceforth in a house apart. The latter, the

Bible says, was buried, not in the mausoleum reserved for royalty, but in the field surrounding it, "because he was a leper."

Whoever, or whatever, may have been the carrier of the plague, a thirteenth-century English chronicler estimated the number of leper-asylums in the Europe of his day at nineteen thousand. The first English one was opened in Canterbury not long after the Conquest. In viewing such statistics, however, allowance must be made for the fact that, in days gone by, leprosy was a somewhat comprehensive term. Numbers of men and women, suffering from this or that skin disease, were liable to find themselves classed as lepers, and treated accordingly.

The decision as to who was and was not leprous did not always rest with the physician. Among the Jews, it was the priest who made the diagnosis, and elsewhere it was commonly decided by public opinion. It is evident from the book of Leviticus that what we call ringworm was, at that time, judged to be leprosy. Although a lazar-house or lazaretto was, strictly speaking, a pest-house for the reception of lepers — *lazar* being Middle English for "leper" — yet the term was later applied to a building sheltering those suffering from any contagious disease. Even nowadays, at seaports, any vessel set aside for purposes of quarantine is sometimes called a lazaretto.

The lazar-houses of the Middle Ages were not hospitals in the modern sense of the word, since in them no attempt was made to check the progress of the disease, far less to find a cure for it. At the same time, all the resources of religion were placed at the disposal of the inmates, in an endeavor to sustain and comfort them in their affliction. They were no longer regarded as so many scapegoats singled out to absorb the shocks of the divine anger. Special religious organizations were started whose members were under vow to dedicate themselves to this particular work of charity. They were called Knights Hospitalers of St. Lazarus, and they made a start in England by opening a hospital at Burton in Leicestershire, henceforth known as Burton Lazars. Each house of this order had its own church, chaplains, and cemetery.

However, not all the known victims were congregated in these leprosariums. Such of them as were at large had to wear a special dress and carry a wooden clapper to give warning of their approach. They were forbidden to enter inns, churches, flour mills, and bakehouses, to make any contact with persons other than lepers, to wash in any stream, or to walk on any public highway.

In the nineteenth century, Europeans, if they discussed leprosy at all, were able to do so with calm detachment. As far as they were concerned, the thing was a sort of museum-piece, of interest only to the historian and the antiquary. But those of them whose missionary calling carried them to Africa, India, China, Japan, and Oceanica came face-to-face with the scourge in all its pristine horror and hopelessness.

In the district assigned to him on his arrival in Hawaii, Father Kamiano soon found that this was going to be one of his greatest heartbreaks. By that time, a government order had been issued for the rounding up of all lepers, prior to their immediate transportation to the settlement in Molokai. Many of the natives resisted to the last, and had to be manacled and carried to the boats by main force. Families were broken up, husbands and wives and children separated the one from the other. And worst affliction of all, for any who really cared for these tragic sufferers, was the knowledge that, in their new home, they were going to live and die bereft of any form of moral or spiritual guidance.

Under the influence of this thought, Kamiano had reached his great decision. That was in 1873 . . . And now, twelve short years had brought him to this.

Well, no matter! The visiting doctor was here, and it would be something to get that over.

"Father, I cannot bring myself to tell you."

These were Doctor Arning's first words, as soon as he had made a cursory examination of the priest's face. Kamiano reassured him. "There is no need to. I have known it for some time."

Then there was silence between them until the doctor went on: "How old are you?"

"Forty-five. It is not easy to die at that age. But no matter."

"Come now, you have some years before you yet."

"You do well to put it like that. Some years — that might mean anything; but, of course, you and I know what *some* means in this case: three at most, possibly two. But no matter."

"But surely, you must have contemplated the possibility of this ever since you came to the island?"

"Contemplated the possibility? No; better say that I glanced at the possibility from time to time, glanced at it as one glances at the prospect of death from the buoyant security of youth and high spirits. We may see this or that calamity playing havoc with those about us, and yet be astonishingly unwilling to entertain the notion of its ever falling upon us. You must know as well as I, Doctor, that the enjoyment of robust health endows you with a firm faith in the stability and immunity of your own body. The suggestion that you yourself may join the long procession of casualties makes no more impression on you than does the blow of a weapon on one who is clad in armor. And, even when the evidence is becoming too strong for this conviction, the optimism in us fights on like a soldier determined to sell his life dearly."

"You must have been in very robust health when you arrived in Molokai," Doctor Arning remarked. And all at once he realized that he knew little or nothing of this priest, whose malady he had just been under the painful necessity of diagnosing. He knew him, as everybody in the islands knew him, as the man who, for the past dozen years, had been devoting himself, single-handed, to the physical, moral, and spiritual welfare of a large community, every single member of which was a leper; nearly a thousand strong it was at the moment. And in those lonely years, the priest had stood by the deathbed, made the coffins, and dug the graves of as many again. But this immense, awe-inspiring item of information had somehow made every other item appear insignificant. It was time to get at some of the other facts, all the same.

"Yes, you have a robust and vigorous frame even yet. Where were you brought up?"

"In Belgium, at a small place called Tremeloo, and on a farm. My father was a farmer. My real name is Joseph de Veuster. When I became a missionary, of course, I renounced my family name, de Veuster, just as I renounced my country. And I exchanged the Joseph for Damien. That is how the lepers came to call me Kamiano. It was the nearest they could get to Damien."

"And were you sent here as a matter of religious obedience?"

"No, I came of my own accord. I hadn't been long out in the Pacific when I heard terrible tales of the plight of these lepers, whom the government, as you know, incarcerated on this island of Molokai. I could not sleep at night for thinking of them. And do you know? Although, when I landed, the actual plight of these creatures turned out to be fifty times more dreadful and revolting than anything I had ever anticipated, the first night I slept under a tree, and slept like a top into the bargain."

"You have never regretted that landing?"

"No, not for a moment. Regrets have just refused to come my way, that is all. When I paid a visit to Honolulu, I was so homesick for my lepers that I could not get back to them quickly enough.

We are strange animals, we human beings — don't you think, Herr Doctor?"

"Truly! But what state were the lepers in at that time, at the date of your landing?"

"In a state of all-around destitution. Everything was bad here; as bad as bad can be: bad water, bad food, bad accommodation, bad clothes, bad sanitation, and, worse than anything, bad habits. So little attention had been paid to the burial of the dead that the cemetery was almost unapproachable. The living quarters were little better. When I officiated in church or visited my flock in their huts, I had hard work to restrain myself from taking to my heels. And yet, the year spent here, dressing sores and stumps as you might say, have been the happiest of my life. We *are* strange creatures."

"But, surely, this sort of sick nursing was hardly what you bargained for when you became a missionary?"

"No, hardly. But, nevertheless, it is in strict accord with the apostolic character. We have the example of our Savior Himself. By practicing bodily healing, He made it plain that His religion was intended to minister to the whole man. His first disciples were endowed with miraculous power over disease. As for the natives of these islands, and indeed for natives generally, this sort of service is in the nature of a restitution. It is something we owe them, in strict justice, as a compensation for the callousness with which they have been exploited by the colonial powers."

"I hadn't thought of it in that way, I must confess."

"No, nor had I until lately; not, in fact, until I had recovered from the shock of this discovery. But I have thought about it since, and the thought has brought me a strange peace of mind. I really feel that there is something worthwhile about the misfortune that has befallen me. I have that satisfaction, over and above the satisfaction that comes from knowing just where one stands and just exactly what the future has in store."

"What do you intend to do?"

"I intend to go on with my work as usual. I still have the use of my limbs, and I must not disappoint my fellow-lepers. You see, we have our annual procession coming off soon. The band is practicing night and day, and I am the conductor. The players have stuck to me, although many of them have only four or five fingers to play with. I must stick to them in my turn. The night cometh when no man can work. Still, it hasn't come yet for me; not exactly. So, *en avant!* I say. Besides, a hundred times over I have told my flock that patience and resignation are possible even for a leper. Mine is now the opportunity of putting decisive testimony to the proof."

∞

Kamiano survived, after a fashion, for four years. He died on April 12, 1889. Shortly before the end, there was a complete disappearance of all the terrible marks with which his face was disfigured. He was buried by the side of the tree under which he had slept the night following his landing. The saddest day of all, in the life of the settlement, was the one on which his body was taken up and transported across two oceans, to be reinterred in his native Belgium.

It was a point of honor with this man never, by word or action, to give his lepers the impression that he shrank from them, or was anxious not to catch the disease. In conformity with this principle, he neglected to take certain precautions. There were other precautions he neglected through ignorance. To be sure, the medical and missionary world has, by now, grown much wiser about leprosy and the leper. But it has done so thanks largely to the stimulus provided by this man's heroism. His was the lot of the pioneer who is privileged to make all the mistakes in order that posterity may not make any of them.

As it was, the conscience of the civilized world was roused by his example, so that the concentrated study of the disease may almost be said to date from his death. In consequence of that study, doctors and nurses and missionaries are no longer terrified into inactivity by the mere sound of the word *leprosy*. In 1897, the superior of a religious body appealed for volunteers to work among the lepers. Six were required, and she received a thousand applications. That was one fruit of what otherwise looked like a fruitless sacrifice.

And in consequence of that study, the age-long superstition that hindered the scientific investigation of the disease has been exploded. It is now known that this is an ordinary, natural complaint; a bacterial disease resembling tuberculosis, and one that is less infectious than tuberculosis. As a result, the old policy of strict and compulsory segregation is being gradually given up. Every effort is now made to encourage the victims to come forward, in the early stages, a thing that many were afraid to do when the threat of the concentration camp hung over their heads. Lepers are now being housed in agricultural colonies, and treated like ordinary outpatients. Already this system has produced a marked falling off in the incidence of the malady. The cure of the complaint is making such rapid strides that it is firmly believed that the scourge will disappear from the Hawaiian group of islands within the space of the next twenty-five years.

In short, the ultimate conquest of this disease is now a certainty. In time it will disappear from Africa, Asia, and the islands of Polynesia, as surely as it has disappeared from our continent of Europe. When that fortunate day dawns, the saying of bygone days will perhaps be recalled: "It is expedient that one man should die that the whole nation perish not."

∞

Aloysius Roche

Aloysius Roche was born in Scotland in 1886. Ordained a Redemptorist priest, he eventually had to leave the order because of poor health, and went on to serve at Most Holy Redeemer parish in Essex, England. There he became known for his wise sermons and his simple, holy lifestyle.

Canon Roche (as he came to be called) tied current events into many of his sermons, showing how we, like the saints, can attain holiness in and through all the circumstances of our lives and our world. His writing exhibits an extensive knowledge of the lives of the saints and speaks of them with such familiarity, warmth, and charm as to bring them close to us, to teach us the simple secrets of their happiness, and to move us to become what God calls us all to be: saints in our own time.